FROM
CIA
TO
CEO

Rupal Patel is a born-and-bred New Yorker now living near London. Her unconventional career as a CIA officer turned serial entrepreneur has taken her from military briefing rooms in jungles and war zones to corporate boardrooms and international stages. As a CEO, leadership consultant, strategic advisor, and coach and mentor, she now helps founders, leaders, and next generation change-makers rewrite the rules of success and become unstoppable. Learn more at: www.rupalypatel.com

FROM CIA TO CEO

RUPAL PATEL

Heligo
Books

First published in the UK by Heligo Books
an imprint of Bonnier Books UK
4th Floor, Victoria House
Bloomsbury Square
London, WC1B 4DA
England

Owned by Bonnier Books
Sveavägen 56, Stockholm, Sweden

facebook.com/bonnierbooksuk
twitter.com/bonnierbooksuk

Trade paperback – 9781788706612
Ebook – 9781788706629
Audio – 9781788706636

A CIP catalogue of this book is available from the British Library.

Cover and prelims designed by Nick Stearn
Typeset by IDSUK (Data Connection) Ltd
Printed and bound in India by Thomson Press India Ltd

1 3 5 7 9 10 8 6 4 2

This book is produced from independently certified FSC® paper
to ensure responsible forest management.

Heligo Books is an imprint of Bonnier Books UK
www.bonnierbooks.co.uk

For, because, and in honour of
my ten thousand.

Contents

Introduction – My Case File   3

Note to the Reader   14

Part One   Thinking Bigger

Chapter 1 Going Deep into Your Identity   17

Chapter 2 Your Field Operations Manual   39

Chapter 3 Your Mission   70

Chapter 4 Your Ops Plan   88

Part One After-Action Review   113

Part Two   Leading Better

Chapter 5 CO-yeS You Are   117

Chapter 6 War Games   137

Chapter 7 Speaking Truth to Power   156

Chapter 8   When the Mission Goes Wrong   182

Part Two After-Action Review   213

Part Three Being Bolder

Chapter 9   Stepping Out from the Shadows   217

Chapter 10 Developing Your Own Tradecraft   244

Chapter 11 Tactical Ignorance   263

Chapter 12 Unshakable   277

Part Three After-Action Review   295

Conclusion: Sustaining Your Ops   297

Acknowledgements   307

A Note on the Dedication   310

Become Unstoppable   312

From CIA to CEO

Rupal Patel

Introduction – My Case File

I spent almost half of my professional life at the CIA and one of the most powerful skills I picked up during my career was a keen ability to analyze everything – including myself – and organize complex information in usable and relevant ways.

My time at the Agency showed me how even the simplest mission can fail because of poor planning, poor analysis, poor support or poor execution. And the crucial role played by planning, analysis, support and execution in any mission success stayed with me even after I left the Agency. It was this analytical toolkit that I brought into my advisory work with corporate leaders and start-up founders. And it is this CIA-inspired toolkit that I share with you here.

The work we'll be doing together in the pages ahead will require you to delve deep into your identity and your backstory, analyze and organize your life and work in new ways, and leverage all that comes with being who you *already* are in the most powerful way possible. We'll be using my tried-and-tested CIA- and CEO-rooted techniques to help you find, honour and unleash your inner powerhouse, and let who you are come out to shine.

But before we get started on you, let me share a bit about my own backstory and how I got here.

I grew up in the eighties in a wonderful Indian-American family that treasured education. My paternal grandfather was a self-taught Sanskrit and English scholar who fought for girls to be educated in small villages in India, building schools and libraries and funding scholarships throughout his life. My father started a book swap service as a child so more rural students could access the books they needed for school and went on to become a surgeon – and a perpetual polymath. My mother came from a line of engineers, doctors and status-quo challengers, and followed in their footsteps. In many ways, my siblings and I were stereotypical New Yorkers born of immigrant parents, steeped in the values of individual progress but with an emphasis on contributing to collective progress, too. We worked hard at school, were expected to excel at everything we did, had our sights trained on Ivy League universities and a clear path of professional accolades set out before us.

We didn't have helicopter parents or a 'tiger mom' – quite the opposite. Our parents infused us with solid values and then left us to make our own choices. They were busy doctors who worked long hours and didn't have time to micromanage, even if they had wanted to. Besides, there were too many of us to keep track of: my older sister, my twin brothers, two sets of grandparents and numerous aunts, uncles and cousins (and the friends of numerous aunts, uncles and cousins) who lived with us for extended periods of time. We would joke that our little house on Staten Island was a mini-Ellis Island, the landing site for hundreds of Indian immigrants who were starting on their own paths to life in America.

Growing up was complicated. I was often embarrassed of my non-whiteness (or made to feel so; 'dot-head', 'camel jockey' and 'towel head' were all pretty regular refrains in my childhood soundtrack) but I was also proud of my smart Indian family. I wasn't allowed to have boys as friends but I managed to sneak out of my house regularly to go clubbing with my cousin. I was 'cool' enough to love hip-hop and reggae (my first job was at an indie hip-hop label) but I was also 'nerdy' enough to be at the top of my high school class. I strained against certain traditions but learned to treasure our expansive definition of family, in which cousins were siblings, and aunts and uncles additional parents.

And because I lived among so many worlds – and so many people – but truly belonged in none; because I had to navigate so many identities – and so many relationships – but fully embodied none; because I was surrounded by so many internal tensions – and so many external ones – but craved nothing more than harmony, I found myself crafting a life within the intersecting parts of many Venn diagrams. Being neither fully one thing nor another made me skilled at ordering chaos and finding ways to connect the previously unconnected.

And I was lucky, too. My parents weren't prescriptive about too much. They set a high bar for me and my siblings, sure, but gave us room to reach it however we saw fit and regularly reminded us to lift others while we rose. And for me, as for so many children of immigrants, living up to my parents' expectations meant doing everything with an eye towards how it would honour their many sacrifices and add another sparkling gem to my life's CV.

And oh, how my CV glittered. Straight As my whole life (even my blood type is A+, for goodness' sake), multiple degrees from prestigious universities, summers volunteering abroad. But I also tried to sparkle my way. I studied political science and interned at the State Department – where I got my first taste of life as a diplomat and expat while living and working in Oman. I didn't become a doctor/lawyer/engineer like everyone expected me to. I charted my own path that drew on my love for data and analysis and languages and complexity, and when the CIA recruited me, it felt like coming home.

I was in my element at the Agency. For six years I was in the eye of the storm – the pointy end of the spear, as we liked to joke – surrounded by brilliant people, working on issues of international importance, demystifying complex information, and living and working in places and with people I would never live in or work with otherwise. After months of training, I was thrown into the deep end. I found myself informing our nation's counterinsurgency strategy in a war zone, experiencing the perils of nation-building while working in the field, earning distinguished service awards and medals for my deployment to a war zone during a critical turning point and advising military and intelligence officers from around the world. In my twenties.

My work was glamorous in the most literal sense. I lived in and travelled to South America, South Asia and Europe. I walked the halls of Western power and decision-making. I advised generals, policy-makers and presidents. And I had fun. So much fun. Not the frivolous, freewheeling kind but the deep fulfilment and sheer joy kind that came from doing work that I cared about and from wiring my brain and my body in new ways.

The CIA trained me for physical combat (driving tactically, shooting rifles and pistols, triaging sucking chest wounds, tying tourniquets) and mental 'combat' (conducting analyses of competing hypotheses, working with foreign liaisons, dealing with difficult interlocutors). Sexy stuff, all of it, that appealed to my inner nerd and my inner badass, and that armed me with the tradecraft – or the seeds of it – that I nurtured, adapted, expanded upon and employed in new and surprising ways in all aspects of my life. It was – and still remains – my ideal career in all of the most important ways and the grindstone that honed so many of my innate skills. Sure, I was brainy and tough before the CIA but the CIA made me brainer and tougher.

And I was lucky to work with some great Agency leaders (who you'll learn more about in part two) who set high standards and expectations, and made it my pleasure to meet them.

But *still*, even still, even in such an ideal-for-me environment I felt an inner calling to never get comfortable. To test myself. To see what more I was made of.

So, I decided to leave the CIA. After the better part of a decade of full-on, 10,000 per cent dedication, I chose my timing and left on a high note. We had found bin Laden, I had just finished helping a new CIA director transition into his role, and it felt like a good time to take a leap into the unknown and pursue a different challenge, expand a different part of me.

So I leaped to London – a city I have always been drawn to – and business school, where I opened my eyes to the big wide world of the private sector, entrepreneurship and international commerce.

And what a brave new world it was!

And what a brave new world it wasn't.

Because once my connecting-the-previously-unconnected muscles kicked in, I started to see parallels between the work I did at the Agency and the way businesses are run and commercial battles are won. I was never going to fit into a corporate mould and I didn't want to waste time trying, so I harnessed my CIA skills and melded them with the skills I had picked up during my MBA to start my own business. I dived into the challenge of building and scaling a real estate investment and development group without any background in the industry and as an outsider. I was a young American woman of colour swimming in a sea of middle-aged white British men and I leaned heavily on my CIA and MBA training – and the 'anything is possible' ethos learned from my family – to make a success of it. Within 18 months, the business was profitable and within a few years my partner and I could have retired in comfort.

But retiring in my thirties is not in my DNA. So I started a consultancy business, advising and training other investors and developers, and then expanded my client roster to include leaders and entrepreneurs of all stripes.

But *still* there was that nagging feeling that I wasn't done yet.

So this time, I sat down like a good little former CIA analyst and studied myself, investigating that voice inside that was telling me there was room for more, that I needed to set my sights on something bigger. I followed the leads.

I looked for the clues. I became my own target. I started tracing my life's journey: its highlights and lowlights; the times when I felt most alive and the times when I felt sucked into a void of boredom and frustration. I looked at what I was doing when the hours felt like nano-seconds and what I was doing when they felt like eons. Who was I with? How was I using my brain? How was I flexing my body? What were my mental and social surroundings?

And from this self-targeting exercise emerged three big patterns: developing an expertise and using it to help smart, growth-oriented people is how I have always felt called to serve; words, written or spoken, are how I have always felt called to share; and nurturing relationships and making new connections are how I have always felt called to engage. These traits made me a natural at the CIA – finding the 'signal' within the intel noise, making sense of complex situations for decision-makers, connecting discrete and disparate bits of information – but how could I use these assets outside of the clandestine world and in a bigger way?

Well, I did what any good agent would do and started to look for targets of opportunity. I found and created ways to share my expertise – to write, speak, engage and connect. I started a few blogs. I spoke at events. I organized salons (not the hair and beauty kind – the eighteenth-century French intellectual discourse kind). And then I did more. And more. And with more focus. And with an eye towards uncovering how I could craft a whole life that was full of the things I have always felt called to do.

And throughout that process I slowly learned to let go of, even forgive myself for, the things I couldn't do or didn't want to do. I never stopped growing and changing, of course, but I stopped beating myself up for what the world told me to view as my contradictions and found ways to honour who I am instead of pressuring myself to become the socially constructed, uni-dimensional ideal of who I should be.

And perhaps most interestingly, I found that when I developed my strengths, instead of obsessing over my weaknesses, my strengths got stronger and my weaknesses became less relevant. And that I could adapt and shape the things I 'should' do in ways that were meaningful and sustainable for me.

I share all this about my past and knowing and honouring who I am as an invitation to you to do the same, and to show you how it is possible. Being true to yourself is not an excuse to be lazy or a call to polish your chinks but a rallying cry to dive deep into your identity and actively engage in living towards your highest potential. To work towards uncovering the truest version of yourself and to be OK with, even proud of, who that person is. Bedazzling your life's CV, as it were, your way.

Here's how we're going to do that.

In part one, I'm going to arm you with a fundamental facet of the CIA mindset: Thinking Bigger and shattering your notions of the impossible. We're going to shake off the mental and emotional dust you've collected along your life's journey and dive deep into your identity, your habits, your rhythms and your environment so you can create new paradigms for how you live, lead and succeed. Thinking Bigger will require you to have some brutally honest conversations with those around you and some brutally honest reckonings with yourself. It won't be easy but I'll be at your side filling you to the brim with can-do confidence that will fuel you towards Mission success.

In part two, we'll build on your 'bigger' foundations to get you Leading Better from wherever you stand and everywhere you go. This means 'bossing it' at work, at home, in your relationships and with yourself by taking a no-bullshit approach to living your values, showing up for what's important and dealing effectively with worry, stress and saboteurs (sometimes disguised as friendlies). As I learned at the CIA, leadership has nothing to do with your title; it has everything to do with your skills and execution. So, I'll be sharing tradecraft tips that will build your confidence, help you speak truth to power and get you back on track whenever you get derailed or distracted by the honey traps life sets for you.

And then in part three, you'll be raring to burst through your chrysalis of bad-assery as I show you how to Be Bolder in everything you do, as I trained myself to do when I left the Agency and built my business career from scratch. I'll show you how to come out of the shadows and let yourself shine, become the highest version of yourself and use tactical ignorance to push yourself further than you thought possible. We'll be finishing up with a final chapter on sustaining your ops, so you can continue your progress and keep your bigger, better, bolder self focused on your Mission.

The tools and tips I'll be sharing with you apply to every stage of your career (and to nearly all aspects of your life) but you have to do the work to see how, when and in which circumstances you can apply them. Whether you are an established CEO, a side-hustle entrepreneur, an early-career professional or somewhere in between, remember to ask yourself 'where else can I use this tool?' to see how much power you can create, how much further and higher you can stretch yourself.

Now buckle up and get ready to soar.

Note to the Reader

Before we get started, grab a journal or notebook or go to www.ciatoceo.com/bonuses and download the worksheets so you have them ready to go for the exercises we'll be doing together.

Part One
Thinking Bigger

Chapter 1
Going Deep into Your Identity

Case File: Owning Who You Are

For much of my life, my external identity was foisted on me. During my childhood, my classmates looked at me as 'the smart Indian girl', no matter that I am a born and bred New Yorker. In college, some of my Indian-American peers labelled me a 'self-hating brown girl' because I had 'too many' black friends. During my war zone deployment, I was the 'civilian analyst' in a sea of military operators. When living and travelling abroad, I have been mistaken for being Israeli, Mexican, Colombian, Guyanese, Polish (!), Pakistani, Dominican, Puerto Rican, Brazilian, Ethiopian and pretty much any nationality that is made up of tanned people who sometimes have curly hair. (I was even mistaken for the amazing Zadie Smith once at a bar in New York. I should have shouted 'Not all brown people look the same, you know!' but I was too flattered by the comparison to care.) This obsession with where to place me is sometimes amusing, sometimes annoying but always followed up by the question 'Where are you *really* from?' after I declare my American-ness.

I seem to confuse people. *You don't act like a typical [insert identity descriptor here].' 'You're not quite what we expected.' 'You have an interesting* [read: non-linear] *background.'* And one of my all-time favourites: *'Your arms are too muscley for a girl.'*

I'm apparently hard to reconcile. An awkward fit. Not easy to place. (That's another reason the CIA felt like such a natural home; in a place where no one fit a mould, everyone fit the whole.)

And for too long, I internalized other people's confusion. There were times – lots of times – when I felt like a weirdo. How could I be mentally tough *and* emotionally astute, analytically sharp *and* creatively gifted, traditional in some ways *and* forward-thinking in others, toned and muscular *and* manicured and be-skirted? But what I realized over time is that none of these things are contradictions. It's only some strange cultural subtext we operate under that expects complex beings to be neatly ordered into simplified, stereotyped categories, when the reality is that we are all messy. The disconnect isn't between us and the boxes we don't fit; it's that the boxes are too limited to begin with.

So don't fall into that trap. Don't force yourself to 'fit' when there is no need. Be who you are, internally and externally, 'contradictions' and all, and own your identity.

Going Deep into Your Identity

As long as you're not an asshole and you accept the consequences of being who you are and how you are, you don't need to fit, or ignore, or downplay anything.

In this chapter, I'll help you release the pressures to 'fit' by showing you how you can revamp your life and your work in ways that honour and leverage your naturally un-fit-able self.

Agents in the field have to immerse themselves in their various identities so that they can live as believably as possible in their cover story; here we'll be looking at *your* identity so that you can live as powerfully as possible in your life story. We'll be digging deep into your backstory so you can concretely identify the environments in which you thrive; using structured techniques to do, dump or delegate the things that fill your days (but might not fill your soul); tapping into your many personas so you can use the right persona for the mission at hand and using profiling systems to illuminate how you can, or need to, restructure your life and work.

This will all be very new to you, so I encourage you to suspend disbelief, just as I did when I joined the Agency. Be open to the extraordinary. And immerse yourself in the exercises and mindset techniques that we are delving into.

Or, in the spirit of the CIA motto, know the truth about yourself and let the truth make you free.

Let's get started.

Backstory

We all have patterns and themes in our lives that can be incredibly illuminating but most of us are too busy doing/achieving/surviving/competing to notice them. That's why the questions in the Backstory exercise below are so important. They force us to stop. Pay attention. And then take action on the things that come up for us.

These are the same questions I asked myself when I was trying to figure out why my CIA to CEO journey felt unfinished in some way. And if you've ever felt like you've got unfinished – or unstarted – business, or that you've got untapped potential crying out for tapping, then delving into your Backstory will help shine a light on where you are sleepwalking and ignite your ability to live more authentically and fully.

You may never have thought about your Backstory in a structured, analytical way, so don't rush this exercise. Find a quiet, distraction-free space where you can sit and reflect for 60-to-90 minutes. Fill in your answers in your notebook or journal, or download a printable version at: www.ciatoceo.com/bonuses.

Backstory Exercise

1) What have been the most fulfilling moments of your career and personal life to date? Try to come up with a few different examples to capture different aspects of

your life. Where were you? What were you doing? What kind of people were you with? How were you flexing your brain? How were you flexing your body?

2) What common themes recur in these fulfilling times? (You were part of a team, you were working alone, you were doing creative work, you were helping others, etc . . .)

3) What can you redesign in your career and life **now** to do more of what fulfils you? What practical things can you change about how and where you live/work to recreate essential aspects of your fulfilling times?

4) What do you know you are good at? What have others told you you are good at? Which of these skills do you enjoy using? How might you make a living from using these skills? The sweet spot is to find an overlap between something you are good at, something you enjoy doing, something people value/will pay you for and something that – ideally – makes a positive impact in your world.

5) What have been the most frustrating moments of your career and personal life to date? Again, try to think of a few different examples. Where were you? What were you doing? What kind of people were you with? How were you flexing your brain? How were you flexing your body?

6) What common themes have you found in your frustrating times? (You didn't have enough clarity about what

you needed to do, you were working alone, there were too many competing stakeholders, you weren't working with driven people, there was no 'buzz' around you, etc . . .)

7) What can you do **now** to mitigate or eliminate these frustrations?

8) Who (a mentor, friendpreneur, partner, etc.) can you work with to help you redesign your career/life so you can do more of what fulfils you and less of what frustrates you?

9) What (financial support, childcare, external accountability, etc.) do you need so that you can start writing the life story you will be most proud of now?

Remember, answering these questions is just the beginning. So sit with your thoughts. Really think about what comes up. Start to consider how you can add to/subtract from what you are already doing. And come back to this exercise and update your answers regularly as your life and career evolve. This is not a one-and-done exercise.

Bringing Your Backstory to Life: 3D your H-L-L-H

When I answered my own Backstory questions, the patterns that emerged showed me that my most fulfilling moments involved developing and then sharing expertise, writing/speaking for an audience that could benefit from my expertise, and engaging and connecting with smart, driven people. But I didn't suddenly abandon everything to start doing these things full-time – the purpose of this exercise isn't to make a precipitous change or become blindly self-obsessed – but I did start to look for and create ways to do the fulfilling things more often and the frustrating things less often. I owned who I am, what I love, sure, but I weaved it into my reality gradually and realistically.

And that's what you can do too. You can start making more decisions based on what is more right for you by weaving more of what fulfils you into your daily life and doing less of what frustrates you. Not a total overhaul, just more, or less. Starting now.

It won't come easily and you'll need to clear space (I know, I know, I'm tasking the already over-tasked!). But you can make better – and structured – choices about what gets your attention and inputs and what doesn't by wielding the H-L-L-H quadrant and the 3Ds (which I'm about to share with you) with power and precision.

Because I get it. As a CEO, in any given hour you might be sucked into the quicksand of your inbox, asked to weigh in on an upcoming board decision, worried about your daughter's cold, wondering whether your company's big deal will go through, thinking about how hungry you are, trying to find 20 minutes for that run you keep putting off, getting annoyed that you have to pee again (what a waste of time all this water drinking creates!), making tweaks to your talking points for an upcoming investor meeting, and, and, and, and . . .

As an early-stage start-up founder, in any given hour you might be navigating between ten different comparison sites to fare-hack your train tickets to visit your supplier next week, waiting for your browser to load the next episode of your favourite TV show while you shovel a ready-meal into your mouth, wondering why your co-founder isn't dealing with the annoying email that just popped into your inbox, worried that your normally-buzzing team Slack group has gone quiet and yelling at the internet connection for being so damned slow when you're paying for 'ultrafast' and, and, and, and . . .

As a driven high-achiever in a new job, in any given hour you might be reading up on recent marketing campaigns, fumbling over your company's bizarre software systems, being pulled into meetings with colleagues and HR, scheduling viewings for new apartments now that your roommate has decided to move out, looking for a venue to host your local alumni gathering next week and wondering whether you've hit the right tone with your workwear because you keep getting looks but that might just be because you're the newbie but what if it's something else and, and, and, and . . .

Holy shit, is it any wonder that so few of us have spare brain cells left for bringing our Backstory to life or living to our potential – or even thinking about what that potential might be – when there's always so much going on? So much to do? So much to think about?

So when I ask you to clear space for what fulfils you, I do so with the full knowledge that you may want to pummel me but I'm here to show you how you, young Agent-in-training, can do it.

Start by making a list of all of the big and small activities that fill your day. It might look something like:

Make/eat breakfast
Get ready
Commute
Assassinate dictators
Meet with sources
Draft intelligence reports
Run counter-surveillance
Pick up kids
Go to CrossFit class
Pay bills
Make dinner
Watch TV
Sleep (with one eye open)

Really tune in and pay attention, track all of your movements and actions like any good analyst would, list everything no matter how much time it takes you (but feel free to leave out those extended showers or illicit liaisons!) and then, put each activity into the following H-L-L-H quadrant:

	High Value	**Low** Value
Love Doing		
Hate Doing		

What you put in each box is a bit of art, a bit of science and totally subjective (this is about you, no one else). High value activities will usually be the things that make you happy, improve your life, make you better, grow your business, enhance your career, contribute to your goals and mission and anything you are uniquely qualified to do. The low value activities will usually be the things that don't have a measurable impact on happiness, improvement, growth or progress, and/or the things that have to get done (like admin) but don't necessarily have to get done by you. And then of course activities you love and hate are exactly that.

Putting some items from our sample activity list into the quadrant might look like:

	High Value	**Low** Value
Love Doing	Drafting intel reports Sleeping	Getting ready Watching TV
Hate Doing	Meeting with sources CrossFit	Commuting Paying bills

And then the next step is to layer the 3Ds – **Do** (tasks you hold on to), **Dump** (tasks you get rid of), **Delegate** (tasks you give to someone else) – on top of this:

Anything in the 'love to do' and 'high value' corner are things that you should probably continue to **do** and that you should invest as much time, energy and money in getting better at doing as you can. (For the doubters among you, yes, you can even get better at sleeping – one-eyed or two – and I know this because Google told me so!)

Anything in the 'love to do' and 'low value' corner you should probably **do** too. We're not automatons and there is so much to say for simple joys that are done just for the pleasure or the relaxation or the mental checking out that they offer, but it might be a good idea to consider decreasing the amount of time, energy and money you invest in these activities unless you are flush with time, energy and money, and can afford to allocate these valuable resources away from the higher value corner.

Anything in the 'hate to do' and 'high value' corner, you could either **swap** with something else that is of equally high value and that you enjoy/love (trading CrossFit for another form of exercise that doesn't include vomiting as part of the workout, for example) or **delegate** these things to someone else. Now, sometimes you will have to continue doing high-value things you hate – life isn't living in our happy place all the time – but by swapping or delegating some of the items in this corner, you'll create more time and energy to do the ones you still have to do.

Anything in the 'hate to do' and 'low value' corner would be good to **dump** or **delegate**, OR make higher value by **layering** a new activity on top (doing glute contractions while commuting, doing target practice while paying bills) if you can find no other way around it. No brainer. No mercy.

Now, I get it, assassinating dictators might never make it onto your to-do list, so here are some more practical examples of how you can apply the 3Ds to your life:

- **DO** things your way:

  If you're a boss whose early morning commute gets you to the office stressed and harried, move the start of your day back a few hours. If running isn't your favourite way of staying healthy, try walking every time you take a phone call and watch the steps rack up. If you struggle to get up with the 5am Club, make it 7am instead. Or do 5am during the week and 9am on the weekends. Life isn't all or nothing. One of my CEO clients moved her morning team meetings from 9am to 10am so she could avoid busy commute times and in doing so took the early morning stress out of her workdays (and her team's, too!). For me, I find exercise for its own sake boring but love being toned and strong, so I do push-ups, chin ups and a lot of walking throughout my day, and ballet,

Pilates and obstacle courses to keep things interesting. I also love being up before dawn (who knew?) but having a toddler and a baby means that my nights and sleep times are never predictable. So I roll with it: sometimes I am up at 4am after my infant's last feed; other days it's 7am when my toddler gets up. Sleep is important so I have adjusted my expectations to honour my reality: I fall asleep when my kids fall asleep and rise when the first of them rises. It doesn't have to be all or nothing.

- **DUMP** the things you hate doing or that add little value to your career or life:
  If you detest 'face time' office culture, don't inflict it on your team just because it's the done thing in your industry. If you hate business networking events and find yourself nursing a drink or running to the bathroom to escape conversation, stop going to live events and find other ways to get the information or make the connections. If there are people in your life who are spirit-sucking energy vortexes, stop spending time with them. Many of my C-suite clients have realized during our work together that they can abandon traditional work practices – daily meetings, five-day workweeks, uniform working hours – without hurting performance. My introverted clients often discover from our work together that they can gain relevant industry knowledge

through podcasts and books and forge connections over Zoom instead of having to go to events in person. And as I've uncovered for myself, I can cut (or at least limit) the time I spend with people who drain me and narrow the topics I discuss with them/what I do with them so I can honour who they are, too (more on this later). Again, it doesn't have to be all or nothing.

- **DELEGATE** one thing that you consistently put off but have to do at work or at home:
  If you always delay having difficult conversations with suppliers, ask your co-founder to have those conversations instead. If renegotiating with your broadband provider gives you hives, hire a virtual assistant to do the dirty work for you. If you're not a PowerPoint savant, put the presentation together in a voice note and then get a graphic designer on Fiverr to create the deck for you. Sharing the load means things will actually get done – and often to a better standard – than if you remain Chief Everything Officer. For me, one of the best decisions I ever made was to hire a part-time PA who fights my customer service battles for me and a VA who does most of my tech admin. I don't have the patience, inclination, temperament or headspace for that stuff but it needs to get done and my assistants are the heroes and she-roes who get it done for me. Phew and phew! Delegation doesn't have to cost a lot of money, either, and I've given you exercises in

Chapter 4 on freeing up funds so you can stop holding onto all of the tedium on your plate.

Doing, dumping and delegating your way through your H-L-L-H quadrant won't suddenly make everything perfect and pull you to new heights of success and fulfilment overnight. But taking thoughtful steps to revamp how you live and work *will* compound over time, and pretty soon you'll find that you have designed a life that is truer to who you are instead of erecting a daily gauntlet that punishes you for who you are not.

You will be stunned at how much time (oh, so much time), mental energy (oh, so much energy) and inner capacity (oh, so much capacity!) these small changes will release. All that cerebral goodness can then be focused on being better at what you care about, on doing things you value and on pursuing *your* mission.

Mission accomplished: space cleared.

> *Executive Order:* As you start doing, dumping and delegating to clear the noise and clutter from your life and honour who you are, you will find it tempting to conflate delegation with abdication. I've done this. All of my clients have done this. Almost every leader I've worked with has done this. And it is an alluring trap that I am warning you about now so you don't fall into it. I repeat: Do. Not. Do. This!

The relief and euphoria you'll feel by giving someone else a task from your pile will seduce you into thinking you'll never have to worry about that task again. False. Just because someone else is now *supposed* to be handling a task, doesn't mean they *will* handle it. You need to make sure things are getting done, even after you are no longer the one doing them. Or as we'd say at the CIA: **trust, but verify**.

Personas

Now that we're on a roll about honouring who you are and you're creating more time, energy and headspace to do more of what fulfils you, let's start exploring how to leverage your many identities. Spies use a variety of personas and aliases for different purposes in different scenarios and it's a powerful tool you can use, too. It's not fakery or falsehood; we're all multi-faceted people whose multi facets get activated or muted in different environments. The trick is to **choose the persona appropriate for the Mission** and then dive deep into that skin.

Let's take your **Success Persona**, for example. Tune into the times you killed it at work, the presentation you nailed, the difficult conversation you didn't shrink from, the moments when you were most unstoppable. What were you wearing? What were you doing? Who were you with? What did you feel? Which of your personality traits were activated? Which new skills might help that persona come out more often? What rituals or clothing choices can get you into your Success Persona more easily? (Do you see echoes of your Backstory in these answers? I told you the patterns and themes were there!)

Elite athletes, stage performers, C-suite executives and high-performers of all stripes put on their Success Personas using tools like visualizations, energizing music, meditation, breathing techniques and physical exercise. So, as you study yourself, start identifying how you get into the best persona – your Parenting Persona, your Negotiation Persona, your Handling-Difficult-People Persona, your Speaking-in-Front-of-an-Audience Persona, etc – for the Mission in front of you.

And remember, you can do the *opposite* with your uglier personas. Dial those babies down, take them off and shed their skin before they take control. Got a Short-Fuse Persona that is holding you back at work or sabotaging your relationships at home? As you feel it slithering up inside you, slip it right back off. Find your Always-Have-to-Be Right persona kicking in during an important conversation? Judo kick it hard and leave it gasping on the floor. (I'll be sharing tips on how to R.E.S.E.T. some of our darker behaviours in Chapter 3 but for right now, just accept that every persona – good and not-so-good – can be as easily taken off as put on.)

You can also adapt your personas for different purposes. If you are an accomplished runner, think of the successes you have had in recent races, times you've beaten your personal best, the muscle tone and strength you've gained through training, and take a few minutes to visualize your triumphs on the track, to feel what it felt like when you beat your last record. Let the flood of success hormones pump you up before you need to be successful in another arena (at work, in an important meeting, as a speaker at a conference). Your Top Runner Persona is a part of you, so don't discard it when you take off your sneakers. Bring it with you in all aspects of your life.

Or if you're a badass contract negotiator and get your clients consistent results, tune into the accolades you've gotten from them, remember the ease and grace with which you handle opposing views and bring that confident mofo with you the next time you have to have a difficult conversation with a spouse or a friend who you normally defer to. Your Master Negotiator Persona is a part of you, so don't discard it when you leave the office. Bring it with you in all aspects of your life (but feel free to leave the corporate-speak behind!).

Or if you're a thoughtful deliberator who takes time to reflect on and understand an issue from all angles before forming an opinion and sharing it, bring that considered approach to your board meetings instead of letting yourself get pulled into the-loudest-voice-wins-the-day posturing. Your Deep Thinking Persona is a part of you, so don't discard it when you enter a room full of spontaneous spewers. Bring it with you in all aspects of your life.

You are not a compartmented person, so leverage that. Tune into your multiple, powerful personas whenever you need to, bringing them with you wherever you go, dialling them up or down and adapting them for the mission in front of you.

Profiling

And finally, no discussion of identities and personas would be complete without a note about profiles. CIA agents create detailed profiles of their targets – what they care about, what makes them tick, their vulnerabilities, their psychological makeup, their personality. You have probably come across some commercial profiling systems like Myers Briggs, Strengths Finder, Love Languages and Human Design in your own career or life.

The beauty of using profiling systems on yourself is that they can help you identify explicit patterns and themes (there they are again!) that you implicitly know about yourself, so why not try them all and create as concrete a picture as possible of 'Target: You'? While no human being is reducible to just one type, each profile test will uncover or confirm some aspect of who you are and you will see patterns emerge that may help enlighten or refine how you live and lead. You may even feel like what you learn brings you back home to yourself.

For example, when I did the Love Languages test, I found out that one of my 'languages' is Quality Time. I used that insight to change how I relate to those I love, of course, but I also put it to work in my business. I hate talking on the phone, checking voicemail stresses me out and being always available interrupts my quality time with my work, myself or my loved ones. So I subscribed to a call answering service that fields all of my work calls and I changed my cell phone voicemail greeting to say that callers should not leave a message because I don't check them; if they want to get hold of me, they can text me or email me. (A founder I advise who adopted my ban on voicemail told me that a lot of people told her they respected her approach and were considering banning voicemail for themselves. What a wonderful side-benefit to living more in alignment with who we are, if by doing so we can enlighten and empower others to do the same!)

It's such a small thing but not talking on the phone or using my voicemail has made my life and work less harried, and it allows me to focus only on the calls I absolutely need or want to make. If I hadn't tapped into my love languages I would never have made these changes or learned that they would serve me as well as they do.

Going Deep into Your Identity

When you start using profiles on yourself, try to use all of your results to inform every aspect of your life. After all, your identity and Backstory – the fundamentals of who you are, what you love, where you struggle, all the patterns – travel with you wherever you go and whatever your mission may be.

> **Executive Order:** Before moving on to Chapter 2, please take time to stop and do the work. You have to be important enough to yourself to invest time in yourself, so don't fly through this book mm-hmm'ing and ah-ha'ing and leave it at that. Put time aside to do the exercises, create the conditions and immerse yourself in the thinking. Now might be a good time to get working. Or the last 20 minutes of your day before you go to sleep tonight, say. But whatever you do, don't passively absorb. Actively engage. That is an order.

Key Intel

- You are complex but you are not a contradiction. Own who you are.
- Trace your Backstory and identify the themes and patterns that emerge so you can start recreating/eliminating the environments where you are at your best/worst.
- Use the H-L-L-H quadrant to regularly review what you are doing and identify what to Do, Dump and

Delegate so it is easier for you to operate at your best more often.

- Identify ways to adapt or adjust your daily activities and responsibilities so they amplify your strengths. Design out as many low-value and energy-sucking activities as possible.

- Develop your many personas and choose the right persona for the mission in front of you. Work on dialling up/down various aspects of your personality based on what the scenario demands.

- Learn from the many personality profiling systems out there and apply the lessons to all aspects of your life; you are not a compartmentalized person.

Chapter 2
Your Field Operations Manual

Case File: How You Show Up

When I was assigned to work in a war zone, a key part of my role was to liaise with military units from across the world. I worked closely with four-star generals, elite Special Forces units, fresh-faced 'grunts' and every rank in between – all of them men. I knew that my gender might be viewed as a weakness or liability so I always showed up as powerfully as I could: I stood tall, spoke firmly, made eye contact and was always well prepared so that no one could question my competence or my presence. But it was my firm handshake that was always noticed and commented on. Every man in the field mentioned it, almost without exception – 'Nice grip,' they'd say, eyebrows quirked and faces full of surprise that li'l ole me could muster the muscle to squeeze a hand with noticeable pressure – and every man I worked with treated me with personal and professional respect.

Now, was that respect all down to my handshake? Well, no and yes. No, because all of the other work I put in created a total picture of confidence and credibility that conveyed I was someone to take seriously. But yes, the handshake was important because it was part of their first impression of me. And first impressions are mercilessly stubborn.

If I had had a wet-spaghetti handshake (or muttered through my briefing, or shrank into myself during meetings), it would have taken a lot more for me to establish my credibility, thanks to confirmation bias. After someone forms an initial impression of us, they tend to see only the things that confirm that impression, so a weak handshake (or speaking softly or blending into the wallpaper) would have conveyed weakness, and that impression of weakness would then poison every other interaction. But because I started out strong – strong handshake, strong voice, strong presence – the teams I worked with in the field interpreted everything through that first impression of strength. Same person, same substance, different potential outcomes because of how I showed up.

So don't dismiss the small stuff. How you look, how you speak, how you stand, everything about your bearing and appearance sends signals about who you are and how the world can *try* to treat you. In this chapter, we'll be working on matching who you are on the inside with how you show up on the outside so that you can become unstoppable.

When conducting clandestine operations, CIA officers are guided by Operations Manuals that set out the parameters and rules by which they should execute their plans. Every agent in the field also needs to develop a keen Situational Awareness (SA) to make sure they don't get blindsided (or captured!) by ignoring the conditions around them. It's important that you create your own Ops Manual to guide how you perform in your day-to-day operations at work and at home, and that you develop Situational Awareness to increase your chances of operational success. What this means in practical terms is that you start tapping into yourself, reviewing how you operate and when, how and where you produce your best. Then adapt and adjust your world as much as you can, taking into account your own work and life realities.

As we go through the process of devising your unique Ops Manual, you will learn how to uncover your Personal Energy Map™, increase your Situational Awareness so that your external surroundings complement and amplify your internal workings, leverage Windows of Opportunity and Go Grey selectively and intentionally, so that you can make a powerful impact with how you show up.

How You Operate: Your Personal Energy Map™

I hate Mondays. It's a bit of a cliché, yes, but the cultural aversion to the first day of the working week is something that I have internalized (to the *Office Space* lovers amongst you, the line 'Looks like somebody's got a case of the Mondays' perfectly captures the dejection and dread we have poured into this poor, innocent day). Even when I was at the CIA and waking up at dawn so I could get to headquarters by 7am was something I looked forward to each day, I would still feel a bit down as early as Sunday morning because Monday was just around the corner.

Consequently, the first thing I did when I became my own boss was to cancel Mondays. I slept until I naturally woke up (which was never later than 8am, I was horrified to find out), dabbled in and out of work and I didn't obsess over getting much done. At first, it felt lazy and self-indulgent and wrong, until I finally realized that – hello! – one of the biggest perks of working for myself was that I get to decide my schedule and I get to define the rules. I had no problem working on Saturdays and Sundays so it was fine – in fact, it was pretty damn freeing – to cancel Mondays and move on.

Although, to be honest, I never cancelled them entirely. I couldn't fully escape my 'good-girl' guilt complex (or maybe it was my immigrant family work ethic . . . whatever it was, it had a fire-and-brimstone-like grip on my psyche), so I made Mondays *mine*. I remade them in *my* image. I limited my expectations for the day and I used it as a warm-up for the rest of the week. What this meant and still means in practice is that I try not to book anything energy intensive on Mondays – be that phone calls, meetings, events, speaking engagements or certain emails – unless I absolutely have to. And if I do, then I limit myself to doing just **one** highly important and energy-intensive thing on my Mondays – and once that thing is done, I am done.

Not everyone can cancel Mondays (or Fridays, or anything after 3pm, or . . .), it's true. But even if you're not your own boss yet, you can still find ways to modify your schedule and adapt your activities according to your Personal Energy Map™ (PEM). Think of your PEM as a, well, map of your energy levels and mental frame of mind during a typical/average week/season/year.

Charting your PEM will require thought and analysis (like much of the work you've already done with your CIA analyst hat on) and begins with tuning into yourself and reflecting on the general patterns that emerge when you ask yourself:

- When in the week do you feel most creative?
- When are you most productive?
- When do you have a head for detail?
- When do you get fed up with minutiae?
- When are you full of energy?
- When do you need a nap?
- What day, or time of day, do you enjoy interacting with others?

- What day, or time of day, do you find yourself desperate to be alone?
- Are there monthly or seasonal variations in your energy levels for different types of activities?
- Are there monthly or seasonal patterns to what kinds of activities you naturally shift your focus to?

Whether you consciously tune into these patterns or not, they are there and they are either helping you or frustrating you, so start being mindful of your own unique rhythms and patterns and make what you do *implicitly* something you monitor *explicitly*.

Top Secret Tip: For all of my fellow uterus owners out there, your PEM will also require tuning into your menstrual cycle, as where you are in your cycle can dictate what types of activities – creative, strategic, detailed, social . . . clandestine! – you feel best equipped to perform at any given time (very broadly speaking, when oestrogen is high, think externally focused tasks, and when progesterone is high, think internally focused ones). Our hormones are a gift we can leverage and incorporate into our PEMs and I've shared some recommended reading in the bonuses at www.ciatoceo.com/bonuses that will help you work in flow with your flow.

> **Executive Order:** Your energy peaks, troughs and seasonality may look very different to the pattern of living and working that you have been shoehorned into since birth and they will be very different from other people's, too. It's OK to be different and 'out of sync' with the rest of the world. Don't fret. Uncovering your PEM will give you the insights you need so that you can find ways to adapt your life's many activities and schedules to work more in sync with your natural alignment. Your PEM will change over time, so be sensitive to when it shifts so you can make any shifts to your life along with it.

My Daily PEM:

So, what can working within your PEM look like in practice? Well, right now, my PEM looks something like this:

Golden hours (when I am most creative and full of energy): 4am to 8am (as long as I've had seven-ish hours of sleep) – this time is dedicated to writing and creative work

Mentally checked out: 8am to 10am

Hungry like a mofo: every 3–4 hours

Needing some me time: 11am (even if just for a warm drink and a snack . . . those Hobbits were on to something with their second breakfasts and Elevenses)

Productivity waves lasting between 40 and 90 minutes: 10am to 4pm

Mentally winding down: 4pm–6pm

Family mode: 5pm–7pm

Tired (and sometimes irritable!): 7pm onwards

My Weekly PEM:

Mondays
Cancelled – as above, with caveats.

Tuesdays, Thursdays
My engaging-with-others energy is highest, so this is when I do my podcast interviews, speaking engagements, business development and marketing activities.

Wednesdays
My anything goes day! A lot of the time I use this day as an 'annoying admin' day to take care of the administrivia and emails I can't bear to do on other days.

Fridays

My helping others energy is highest, so Fridays are reserved for executive clients, running my Entreprenora boardroom, doing advisory calls and hosting workshops. This is also when I am at my most emotionally expansive, so perfect for extended conversations with loved ones.

Saturdays

I am still winding down from the week so I do some light and enjoyable work for part of the morning (writing, writing and writing).

Sundays

Total chill time and lazy time. Even if I'm up early, I usually indulge in whatever I feel like doing: reading for long hours (assuming my kids let me!), making breakfast a big waffle-filled event and spending quality time with my husband and daughters.

My monthly/seasonal PEM:

September – November

I am super high-energy (it's the Lisa Simpson in me who loves the 'back to school' season) so I do all of my planning, strategy and big-picture thinking activities here as well as a ton of events and writing.

December

This is my month equivalent of a Monday so I plan to do very little that is high energy or mentally intensive unless I want to. It's also my birthday month so another reason (excuse?) to pull the shutters down.

January – February

This is when I put plans in motion for executing the big picture and strategy, aligning my goals, training my team, getting in any additional support and making tweaks to my PEM (if needed) for the year ahead.

March – June

I am solar powered, so these are the months when I execute, execute, execute on big plans and focus on connection-making with others.

July – August

Spending quality time with family and winding down before the September cerebral push.

Now, this isn't a perfect science. My PEM is of course always head-butting against reality, other people's expectations (and their PEMs) and the time, energy and resource requirements of everyday life as a CEO, parent, advisor, mentor, speaker and writer. We all wear many hats and there are always other stakeholders who want to make tweaks to our PEMs. That's just life. But the key is to create boundaries around what we will let flex and what we keep fixed.

For example, if your fitness is a major priority for you, your gym time becomes fixed and non-negotiable and the rest of your daily activities can flex around that protected workout time. If you're constantly the go-to person at work for organizing social events but want to commit more time to the charity you volunteer at, then you can fix the number of hours you give to work-related extracurriculars and the rest of your free time can be flexibly devoted to your volunteering. If you are constantly feeling the guilt-pull of spending more time with your kids while working from home, you can fix the time you will be 100 per cent focused on them without multitasking (6–8pm, say) and then your work activities can be flexibly organized around that.

The other key is to not be all-or-nothing. Your PEM will never, ever get to call all the shots 100 per cent of the time but knowing what it looks like will allow you to make detours and then come back on track. It will show you the parameters of your natural, optimal performance cycles so that when you can't work within them, you can work consciously outside of them. This framework will guide you to be more thoughtful and creative about how you break down your work and do things in a more PEM-centric way.

For example, if you are not an early bird but your work requires you to start your day at dawn (like mine once did), you might try to push important meetings or calls to later in the day. You could ask your assistant to protect the mornings so you're not interrupted while you warm up for the day. You might minimize the number of mentally taxing things you do early on.

If your mind starts to hibernate with the onset of winter but you work in an industry where your sales and activity ramp up at that time (most retail businesses face this November/December seasonality), you might share your workload with other team members for a short time. You could temporarily hire some help at home to free up energy. You might give yourself a 'just-tough-it-out' talk and reward yourself when you do just tough it out. You could go all guns blazing three days a week and take two days off, or go all guns blazing for three hours a day and then shut down.

If you are most creative during the first week of each month but that is the same week your boss needs you to submit a monthly report, you could ask your boss if you can submit it during the second week instead. (Would your boss really mind? Before you assume anything, have you asked?) You could spend half of each day that first week doing creative work and the other half doing the report. You could get someone else on your team to help you (perhaps in exchange for your helping them work according to their PEM). You could leave a few hours at the end of each day for your creative work. Or you could gee yourself up to get the report done by Wednesday so you can have all day Thursday and Friday for the creative stuff.

It doesn't have to be all or nothing. It's about finding creative solutions, big or small. Something as simple as standing up when I give a virtual talk or host an event post-7pm when I am usually in my tired-and-irritated time totally transforms my energy and pumps me full of life. Small thing, big impact.

Because, let's face it, the world doesn't owe it to us to make our lives easy or conform to our plans (or PEMs!). But we shouldn't let the world call all the shots either. We can all make big or small adjustments that take at least some of the friction away. Work within your PEM when you can and use your imagination when you can't.

Executive Order: You'll hear me say this again and again but please do the work. Your PEM is one of the most powerful tools available to regain sanity and clarity in your life but the magic can only happen if you take the time to answer the questions I've shared with you above. Whether in a journal or notebook, get your PEM down on paper and integrated into your life.

Your PEM is a foundational part of your Ops Manual, so now that you've tuned into it, let's take things up a notch to make sure important parts of your identity don't become operational casualties of your day-to-day routine.

Golden Hours and Paying Yourself First

Golden Hours are often talked about in productivity circles as the best times to get shit done. These are the times in your day (or week or month or season or year) when you are mentally on fire, full of energy and utterly unstoppable. The fire can last for forty minutes, four hours or four months and we are usually told to use this supercharged time to supercharge our productivity. But productivity is too often something that is dictated *to* us instead of *by* us (even CEOs have investors, shareholders, board members, family members who demand a piece of us). And nothing deadens the power and energy of the Golden Hour jet plane more than the feeling that someone else is steering that plane for us, and that we are squandering our best time to pursue someone else's agenda. But just because expectations and demands are inevitable, letting them intrude on Golden Hours doesn't have to be!

So, why not pay yourself first before thinking about being productive in the traditional sense? Why not do what you love, what you care about, what fuels you mentally, intellectually, spiritually and/or physically during your protected

Golden Hours before opening the door to the world? Why not redefine what productive looks like by factoring in who you are as a whole human – with passions and a body and mind and spirit that need tending to – before reducing yourself to your work-iest parts?

For me, redefining productivity means using and protecting my Golden Hours for creative work before I even think about opening up my email or doing anything else. But – reality check! – sometimes other pressing demands need to be addressed in this precious time because if they are not, I will procrastinate myself into a heart condition.

For example, as the head of multiple businesses, sometimes I need to put my Boss Lady pants on and do some good old-fashioned money management and accounting. But god, how I hate reviewing my monthly P&Ls. They take only about 30 minutes of my time to look over, but the thought of doing them fills up multiple days' worth of mental and emotional space. So, I hack my internal ops from time to time and let P&L reviewing intrude upon my Golden Hours once a month. On those days, paying myself first actually means doing the P&Ls first because even though they don't make my soul sing, once they are out of the way, an unnaturally large burden is lifted and then my soul can do arias for the rest of the morning.

Top Secret Tip: Whatever your version of P&L review looks like, if you schedule in a regular and repeating time to take care of it, you will take a lot of its exhaustive power away. Instead of the energy drain of wondering/worrying when you'll get around to doing it, decide that every second Tuesday from 6am to 6.30am you'll file your expense reports, say. Or every Monday, Wednesday and Friday from 10am to 11am you'll go to the gym. Or on the first of every month you'll do your business development calls, etc ... Decision fatigue is a real thing, so defang mental-energy-sucking tasks and reclaim precious headspace and energy by putting recurring tasks in a neat little scheduled box.

It doesn't have to be all or nothing. (I've said that before, right?) But we can protect our Golden Hours most of the time – and make sure we pay ourselves first during those Golden Hours most of the time, too.

For one of my clients who's a mid-level manager at a large tech firm, this means spending 30 minutes playing the piano (something that fuels his spirit but had been sacrificed at the corporate altar) on *most* days before he opens up his laptop to do work.

For a serial founder and CEO in my Entreprenora Boardroom, this means carving out 20 minutes to walk her dog or do some gentle breathing exercises (activities that calm her racing mind but don't conform to traditional productivity metrics) on *most* mornings before using the rest of her Golden Hours to get strategic work done.

For a friend-preneur who is an accountant-turned-investor-turned-coach-turned-farmer, this means playing video games for a few hours on *most* days (a source of joy that pumps her full of creative and competitive juices but looks nothing like 'real' work) before she peeks at the mentally and physically demanding day ahead.

Protecting our Golden Hours and Paying Ourselves First is so important because how we live our days is, of course, how we live our lives. So, we owe it to ourselves to do what makes life worth living before we sit down to make our living. We owe it to ourselves to read the books, play the games, pursue the hobbies, tick off the bucket list items now instead of waiting for some mythical 'when' in the future. When we do so, when we bring more of what we love into our daily lives in big and small ways, we'll find that the mythical future can be a reality *now* and – added bonus! – we'll have more patience and energy to do the things we have to do, or need to do, or 'should' do.

So don't forget about what you care about. Don't discard the fun. Don't neglect the many other facets of your many-faceted self. You might not be able to pay the bills as a prima ballerina or pianist or writer or gamer or [insert something you love doing here] but you can pay *yourself* first and do these things each day during your protected Golden Hours. You owe it to yourself – to the person and personas you are beyond your titles and external labels – to do so.

Executive Order: You will resist this. I know it. You will tell yourself that you'll pick up the paintbrush or the flute or the book or the running sneakers *after* you get your work done, *after* you take the kids to school, *after* you do the dishes (why is housework so damn alluring as an alternative to looking ourselves in the face?), *after* you get the promotion, after, after, after. Well, I think you know as well as I do how often we make good on those 'afters'. So here is your Executive Order to pay yourself first starting now. Experiment with it. Warm up to it. Start slowly if you need to. Just take your first ten beautiful, shiny, uninterrupted minutes and do something just for you. Drink a cup of coffee while it's still hot. Read that book. Start writing that book. One sentence, one page, one sip. Make it so small you can't say no. And then do a little more the next day, and a little more the next, and a little more the next until you get used to how it feels, how good it feels, how enlivening it feels to treat yourself as the most important priority for your day.

Situational Awareness

Being thoughtful about where your time goes, protecting your Golden Hours and Paying Yourself First are so important because otherwise you can become blindly – and blithely – 'white' about your career and life. Let me explain.

Before I went to a war zone, my pre-deployment training included a stay-with-me-forever dose of Situational Awareness (SA) training that fine-tuned my sensitivity to pretty much everything. The aim of the training was to make sure my fellow trainees and I grew accustomed to scanning our environments for potential threats and avoiding sticky situations. After all of the scenarios we played out, we were taught to reflect on what colour we were operating in at various points in the exercise: white for 'tuned out/oblivious', yellow for 'relaxed awareness', orange for 'focused awareness', red for 'high alert' and black for 'in shock/frozen'. (In one particularly harrowing exercise that I'll share later, I went 'black' almost instantly and it is not a colour I ever want to operate in again.)

Most people go about their days in a 'white' or 'yellow' state. Hell, many people live their whole lives in 'white'. But that is not for you. We are training that out of you. Because we've already got you turning inward and becoming consciously aware of who you are, how you operate and what you need to show up as your best. So now let's look outward at your physical environment and develop the SA part of your Ops Manual so you can smooth the friction in your day-to-day operations and move fluently and fluidly along the SA colour spectrum.

It's no secret that our external environment has a massive impact on who we are and how we feel. Without realizing it, the stresses, the energy, the people, the sounds, the smells around us all combine into one big experiential ball that affects our mood, our performance, our productivity, our success and our happiness.

In the field, tuning into these external elements and noticing changes to the norm is a signal that something is off, a red flag telling you to go, well, 'red'. And we need to be just as sensitive to our surroundings in our daily lives so that we are attuned to any changes that occur and can then tap into the persona best equipped for the new scenario OR adapt the operational activity – and our operational colour – to best match the new environment.

For example, I know that I always tighten up when I walk into soulless conference rooms. So, to perform at my best in that environment, I tap into my Success Persona, do some deep breathing to relax and mentally review success moments to bring me back to myself and get ready for the conference room conversation. In this way, I move myself from a potentially paralyzing 'red' state to a more productive 'yellow'.

I know that I am best at polishing off tedious admin tasks when there is noise and distraction around me, so if my once-quiet working environment becomes flooded with noise (my husband comes home, our daughters start shouting, the song on the radio gets groovy) then I shift gears from deep concentration work to paying invoices or sending emails.

Situational awareness is all about being finely attuned to yourself and to your environment, so you can change the things in your control (your preparation, your behaviour, your activities, etc) to keep your head in the game and feel and do your best more of the time, whatever the conditions. Tuning into the relationship between your environment and how you perform can also show you what to change in your physical surroundings so you can unlock a better you. Here are some real-life ways to use SA to adjust your work (and home) environments:

Play around with smells

Some of us are more attuned to our olfactory sense than others, so think about what smells you can introduce into your space, tailored for the tasks you conduct in it. For example, energizing smells like citrus for spaces you want to be high energy in (a home gym or family room perhaps) and relaxing smells like lavender for spaces in which you want to feel calmer (a bedroom, say, or maybe your work space). Human beings have used scents for millennia to create mental and physical benefits, and there's plenty of scientific research to show how smells affect energy, performance and cognition.

Play around with lighting

Think about what colour of light you prefer and about different sources of light (adding a candle in an already lit room can really warm up the feel of the space, for example). If you hate the fluorescent bulbs in your office, consider desk lamps. Think about sources of natural light and sunshine. The benefits of including natural light in our spaces are numerous and well documented; work spaces are no different.

Play around with visuals

Create the right visual atmosphere for yourself by thinking about and adjusting what you see: photos, artwork, quotes, colours, whiteboards, shelving, etc. Make your environment look like you need it to, so you get the most emotional and mental benefit. Rearrange your desk so it faces a window, declutter, put thought-provoking quotes on your walls, use more aesthetically pleasing whiteboards (I use frosted glass whiteboards because I hate the sterile look and feel of traditional white plastic ones), pin up pictures of your enemies with targets on them or just change the colour of the walls. You know what looks pleasing and/or motivating to you, so bring an attention to visuals and lines of sight into your spaces.

Play around with air

Air temperature and air quality is so important and studies have shown that working in more comfortable temperatures enables us to perform better. What is comfortable is of course subjective. Some of us (like my husband) need it to be a cool 18 degrees, while I can't think properly if it's less than 21. In shared spaces, compromise if you have to (in our house, sometimes the temperature is set at 21 and my husband wears t-shirts or we keep it at 18 and I layer up). Air quality is also important so make sure you ventilate regularly and add some plants to help take out some of the nasty toxins that build up in indoor spaces.

Play around with sound

Whether you prefer Mozart or the wind tunnel sound of espresso machines, think about the levels and qualities of noise you need to keep your subconscious brain happy. I usually go for silence or sounds of nature (but not water sounds, as they make me want to pee!). I do best with low-volume classical music when I'm working but pop music when I'm cooking. Think about the aural environment you need for the task in front of you and adjust accordingly as best you can (headphones can be your best friend if you work in an office, especially if you are more introverted and go physiologically 'red' from noise and stimulation but can't retreat to a quiet space).

Play around with texture

Our poor lives are so hard surfaced and corner edged these days that we've lost touch (pun intended!) with how easily we can make adjustments to bring more softness and texture into our lives. From sitting on balance balls to standing barefoot at a standing desk, there are endless options for engaging your sense of touch even at work. Can you add a small rug to your cubicle floor? Can you bring in a throw blanket or cushion to use at your desk? Can you order nicer pens that don't leave welts in your fingers? Or order a flak jacket that doesn't squash your boobs? (Those things were definitely not designed for anyone with curves!) Think about the hundreds of things you touch or put on each day and how you can add texture and comfort . . . without needing to show up at the office in your PJs.

Have fun with this. Experiment. Iterate. See what works. See what doesn't. Pay attention. Flex your SA muscles. And play around with what you do and don't need to change. You don't have to conduct an expensive overhaul. Small and thoughtful tweaks can make a big and lasting impact.

Windows of Opportunity

The next piece of your Ops Manual toolkit is to develop your ability to see and leverage Windows of Opportunity. In intelligence operations, these windows are those fleeting moments when the stars are aligned, the weather is clear, the patrol is transitioning, the team is in place, the messaging is taking hold and the boots on the ground can move unimpeded or with less friction, giving the operation a greater chance of success.

In our daily lives, we need to keep an eye out for these rare and optimal conditions too, and when we find ourselves within them – or find them within ourselves – the key is to move like hell before the window closes.

The window can be as small as a 40-minute nap that your newborn takes each day during which you can get something important done or as big as a chance to put yourself forward for promotion during a company merger. It can mean launching that rocket when the atmospheric conditions are right or riding a productivity wave to get through piles of work. It can mean selling your business while the market is hot or travelling the world before starting your new job.

Or it can be something as profound as sensing when a window is opening up inside of you. When you feel suddenly ready to attack a task you've been putting off, you need to go for it. When you listen to a podcast that spurs you to act, you need to act. When you hear about a book or an event that sounds perfect, you need to buy the book or get the ticket. The passion, the flair, the flame, we all know it never lasts. So move when the spirit moves you. Don't keep it waiting.

Because all windows eventually close. And you don't want to be left wondering what could have been – who you could have been – if only you had noticed the breeze rustling your hair while that window of opportunity was still open.

Going Grey . . .

And finally, let's talk about 'going grey'. This is spy-speak for looking and acting in a way that blends you into your surroundings. But for our purposes, it's less 'become a part of the furniture' and more 'show up as the most powerful version of yourself for the context you're in'.

The world is a superficial place. I wish it weren't so – and you might too – but it is only in fantasy land that substance always wins out over style. And the world isn't a meritocracy either. We can all probably cite more examples than we'd care to list of less-than-qualified people landing positions of influence. Or examples of two equally qualified candidates being ranked by intangible traits: presence, charisma, like-ability, gravitas, a certain *je ne sais quoi* . . . How we look and carry ourselves affect how people judge us, that is not a revelation. But taking time to be thoughtful about how you look and carry yourself can be life changing and is an integral part of your Ops Manual. Because there is a fine but critical balance you need to strike between standing out (for the right reasons) and blending in.

Now, I'm not an image consultant or professional stylist but as a woman who has consistently operated in hyper-alpha environments, I've always had to navigate that balance carefully. I've had to make sure I come across powerfully but – double standard alert! – not too powerfully for any fragile egos in the room. I've had to project competence and confidence but not in a 'bossy' way. I've had to fit in with the guys but not erase or ignore the fact that I'm a gal.

Some things I do naturally mean I blend into alpha environments anyway. I have a firm handshake, I look people in the eye, I stand tall, I take up space. And some things I do naturally make me less likely to blend in. This doesn't mean I have to change who I am but it does mean that I need to be thoughtful about how I show up so that others see me the way I want to be seen in that context. And you can too, using all of the work you've done in this chapter as a guide, and by making tweaks with the help of friends, experts or books you trust so you **always show up as powerfully as possible for the context you are in.**

How you need or want to show up will be different based on your industry, background, goals and the specific contexts in which you operate but some aspects that would be good to explore include:

- Posture
- Voice projection
- Clothing and grooming
- Presence/taking up space
- Eye contact
- And of course, handshakes (see Case File, above)

All this 'small stuff' matters and I've added a few recommendations at www.ciatoceo.com/bonuses that will help you refine how you show up so that you project on the outside the power and competence you know is on the inside.

...But Not Going Away

Now, no discussion of blending in, showing up and standing out would be complete without talking about the Mammoth in the Room for women, or what I call the 'too much/not enough problem'. The research-backed TM/ NE problem is the penalty that women confront simply for existing or not blending in enough. Pretty much every state of being or activity will be labelled by some mouth-breathing knuckle-dragger – and they exist at all levels of every organization – as 'too' something or 'not enough' of something else. *'Too ambitious'/'Not driven enough' 'Too masculine'/'Not tough enough' 'Too pretty'/'Not fuckable enough' 'Too sensitive'/'Not maternal enough' 'Too A, B, C'/'Not X, Y, Z enough'* and on and on into infinite infuriating varieties. (The problem exists for people of colour, too; for anyone else who's felt judged because of how you chose to navigate the TM/NE problem of being 'too ethnic'/'not true to your roots enough', I see you.)

Because of stubborn social conventions that still view women's full participation and representation in the world of power, decision-making, authority and life in general as a quaint, niche idea, women are scrutinized and dissected for our appearances and our behaviour at ridiculously higher rates than men (and I can only imagine how much harsher the scrutiny if you're gay/non-binary/trans). Who we are and how we appear is considered fair game for all manner of hurdles and expletives to be thrown our way.

I know this from experience. I know this from the experiences of every single woman I know. I know this from the reams of research and bias studies that have been done on the topic. And I know this from the reams of research and bias studies that have not been done on the topic because women are not deemed worthy of researching or studying beyond a certain point.

So while you are working on how you show up, remember, 'going grey' is not about shrinking away or living a lie as someone else; it's about tapping into *your* badass persona so you can **own** your place in the room, in the field, in the office, in the halls of power or wherever you are without apologizing for being there, or letting others question your presence there.

Use the fact that you're *not* 'grey' and that you *do* stand out as an asset. Call attention to things that others don't see. Be a role model for others who look like you. Use your unique position to lift those behind you. Being the 'only' in the room can be a blessing (if also a burden) so don't efface yourself to keep your seat at the table. You can be 'too much' or 'not enough' or everything in between, but at the end of the day, who cares? If you're showing up as your best, most bad-ass self, then what other people think of you is simply none of your business.

Key Intel

- How you show up matters. Work on it.
- Charting your Personal Energy Map™ will help you uncover how you naturally operate during the day, week, season and year, and show you where you can adjust your routines and tasks so they are more aligned with your natural rhythms.
- Identify when your Golden Hours are and protect them with your life.
- Pay Yourself First each day before you get sucked into the world's agenda for you.

- Use Situational Awareness to reshape your physical environment so that your many spaces and touchpoints support who you are and what you need to do in that space.
- Look out for and take advantage of Windows of Opportunity; they don't last forever and you may never get another one.
- Find the right balance between going grey and standing out in the contexts in which you operate.
- Don't conform or give in to the double standards you face; use being 'different' as an asset and challenge conventions with your powerful positive example.

Chapter 3
Your Mission

Case file: Following the Leads

At the CIA, our core mission was to protect our country from threats. On the ground, this meant many things: collecting intelligence, producing objective analysis, conducting covert actions and safeguarding secrets. Straightforward, yes, but not particularly easy.

Because missions are funny things. In retrospect, they seem clearly bounded and cleanly executed, but in real-time they are an evolving mess that requires a let's-make-the-best-of-this-shit-show-so-we-can-move-in-the-general-direction-of-our-strategic-goals-as-we-figure-things-out-on-the-hoof approach.

And that's how it is for personal missions too. And that's how it's been for me. When I first started thinking about my Mission (or purpose or calling – that thing that would give life to my life), I didn't have a clue what it might be. But I didn't stop everything to figure it out. I took care of all of life's practical stuff (building a business, paying the bills, saving money, washing my underwear, calling my family) but I never stopped looking for signs. Something would come to me and then leave. Ideas would guide my hand and then drop it. Thoughts would plant clues and then run away.

So I tried different things: jobs, activities, businesses, ways of living, arenas for learning and paradigms for leading. I tuned into my personas, my PEM, my Backstory – all that good stuff we've done so far. And I looked inward to guide my experimentation until I finally uncovered what was important enough to me to be my Mission.

But it took a long time. In some ways, it took 40 years of conscious and subconscious work. But for at least five of those years I asked myself the big questions, paid attention to the answers, put the pieces together internally and made my life ready externally (one small bit at a time) so that I could live my Mission on a daily basis whenever I happened to uncover it. Five years – or forty – as an impatient person with impatient goals in an impatient world. It wasn't easy, but it was worth it because without those five years, I would have spent the rest of my life wondering. Without those five years of frustration – of having to do awkward things, of knowing there was something bigger but not knowing what that was, of living in internal frisson and external expectation – I would never have found what I needed to find.

It's so big and so subtle sometimes, our uncovering of our missions. But we have the seeds in us. We just need to tend to them. To take them seriously. To nurture them. And then, when we find that they've bloomed, or just started to bud, to guard those blooms and buds with all we've got.

But we also have to remember that our Mission can be serious without becoming sombre. That it can be something but not everything. That it is heavy but we can hold it lightly. That it has meaning but can mean nothing at all to anyone else but us. And that it's OK if no one else notices, or pays us for it, or pays any attention at all.

Are you willing to look for and follow the leads to find your Mission? And when you do, will you choose to accept it?

To help you uncover your Mission (or Missions), in the pages ahead I'll be introducing you to the Intelligence Cycle and showing you how to use it to sift through your inner sands and bring what matters to you into your life each day. From there, we'll craft a mission motto that will help remind you of your forward and upward path. Don't get bogged down in how big or small or outlandish or internal or confused or concrete any of this might be. Just be willing to explore and experiment and give it a go.

You are the boss here. You decide what's important. And you decide the nature, direction and intensity of your Mission. We'll be building on the themes and insights you've started uncovering in previous chapters, so play around with this. Following the leads takes patience and experimentation. Very rarely, if ever, are intelligence operations blessed with straightforward here-is-the-answer moments – the environment suddenly changes, friends become foes (or vice versa), goals evolve, results take their own time – and uncovering your Mission won't be cut and dried either.

So in the spirit of exploration, openness and curiosity, let's get you thinking about your Mission and unearthing the clues that might be buried inside you.

The Intelligence Cycle . . . and You!

Put on a bib, dear reader, because things are about to get juicy. You've done a lot of hard, meaningful work analyzing yourself like you may never have done before and now it's time to put all that insight to good use. Because knowing who you are, shaping a life that honours that and clearing space and time can feel somewhat directionless if it's not moored to something bigger: your Mission.

One of the many incidental benefits of working at the CIA was the inherent bravado and nothing-can-stop-us attitude that infused our missions. When I served overseas, the discussion was rarely 'We can't,' but often 'How can we?' There is something refreshing and freeing about being so boldly confident and can-do and about persisting even when the results aren't guaranteed.

And what I developed by swimming in this self-assured sea, and then tempering it with my own mixed perspective, is what I like to call an 'enlightened swagger': internalizing that 'anything is possible' (the swagger) while owning the truth that my Mission doesn't have to be an in-your-face endeavour (the enlightened part).

So, be bold about what is possible for you (more on that in Part Three) and give the nay-sayers a loving, enlightened finger (or two) on your way to wherever you aspire to go. Make your Mission yours. Go for what you care about in your way, on your terms and with your values as a compass. Make it what you want without a sideways glance at what it 'should' look like.

Where are you going exactly? Well, only you can answer that, but if you've never given it concrete thought, we're going to use the Intelligence Cycle to get you on your way. This is a handy little piece of structural machinery that I slotted into when I was working at the CIA.

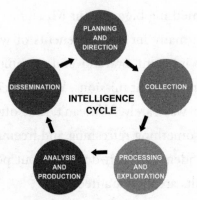

Your Mission

The Intelligence Cycle has five components – **planning, collection, processing, analysis** and **dissemination**. My job was to work on the analysis bit and man, did I relish that job. I was up to my elbows in rivers of intelligence, panned the sand from the gold, then penned finished intelligence reports that were reviewed and refined until they glinted with insight and depth for our most important customers: the President, Cabinet officials, military leaders, Congress and policy-makers at every level of government.

Now, the President of the United States might not be asking you to make sense of the tribal divisions in a foreign locale and what they mean for US interests but you can use the same structured process of the Intelligence Cycle to make sense of what *you* care about and what that might mean for *your* interests and *your* Mission. The work we do within the Intelligence Cycle will then lead very nicely into Chapter 4, where we'll formulate your Ops Plan and pull together the Ops Team that will help make your Mission a reality.

In our adaptation of the Intelligence Cycle, the **planning** part is the most straightforward so we'll cover it fully now. Normally, senior intelligence officers get a directive or a question (from the President, say) and they plan what resources they'll deploy to collect the information needed to respond. For our purposes, **your directive** is to uncover what your Mission might be and your **plan** (well, *my* plan for you) is to deploy my Three Ideals – ideal day, lifestyle and legacy – to collect the essential information you need.

Your **collection** efforts will entail gathering all of the qualitative and quantitative information you can on the key components of your ideal day, ideal lifestyle, and ideal legacy so you can **process and analyze** the 'intel' collected into a usable form. Then you'll **disseminate** your analysis to the relevant stakeholders (in this case, the President probably doesn't care but you and anyone else who might need to get involved in making your Mission a reality will).

The Cycle in Action: Collection – The Three Ideals

Your Ideal Day

It's sometimes easier to dig into big questions like 'What is my Mission?' by thinking in extremes and ideals. So let's start with your ideal day.

Take 60–90 minutes to construct your ideal day, writing down *in detail* what it looks like. Get all of your senses involved: where are you living, what time do you wake up, what is outside your window, what sounds can you hear, what is the temperature, what are you eating, who are you with, how are you dividing your time, how are you flexing your brain, how are you flexing your body, how are you feeding your stomach, how are you fuelling your spirit, what can you smell, feel, touch, taste and see . . . Make it a fully immersive experience and GET SPECIFIC – I'm talking zip codes, portion sizes, thread count, the works! Write everything down.

Your Ideal Lifestyle

Now let's go bigger and look at your Ideal Lifestyle. Again, in a 60–90-minute uninterrupted block, think of all the big and small things that you've told yourself over the years that you want to be, do, and have and write it down. What skills do you want to master? (For me, it is to become more fluent in Spanish so I can deliver events in the Spanish-speaking world.) What are you doing with your 'work' time? (For me, it is writing and speaking.) What are you doing with your 'play' time? (For me, it is travelling and connecting with loved ones over long meals that I haven't cooked!) What kind of house are you living in? (For me, 'home' is a few different places.) What things do you own? (For me, it's not much. A mortgage-free house and car that fit my family, some stylish and comfortable clothes, and furniture made by a craftsperson I can visit in their workshop.) How are you contributing to your immediate world? (For me, it is by being fully present with loved ones instead of multi-tasking my life away.) And how are you contributing to the broader world? (For me, it is by making a positive impact at scale.)

And remember, there are no right or wrong answers so please be as expansive and can-do as you can. It takes just as much effort to think big as it does to think small. Construct a vivid idea of what you want so in the next chapter and onwards we can create a plan to get you there.

Your Ideal Legacy

Now let's get even bigger. Thinking about your legacy might feel overwhelming but all complex things are simple at their core. Answering just four questions will get you a long way towards uncovering what you want your legacy to be:

- What do you want people to say/feel/think at your funeral?
- What specific impact do you want to have made during your life?
- What do you want to be remembered for?
- What would *you* be proudest of?

That's it. No long agonizing process, just four simple questions to help you towards uncovering your Mission and what you want to leave behind.

So how does all this idealizing get you closer to uncovering your Mission? Well, the elements that make up your ideals point like a laser to the things you care about when you are mentally unfettered (we are talking ideals here after all!). They show you what you value when you are thinking expansively. And what you care about and what you value will often point you in the direction of your Mission. (And give you a reality-check-sized slap in the face about where you might be letting yourself down.)

To make this more concrete, let me share with you the most recent iteration of what came out of these exercises for me (I regularly check up on my Three Ideals and you should, too, to see if they have changed as life and priorities evolve):

My Ideal Day: Waking up at 5am after a good seven- to nine-hour sleep, using my Golden Hours for creative work (and indulging in a warm coffee in a quiet house!), then waking our kids and having breakfast as a family before taking them to school. After this, I check in with my team and set them up for their day. I plan or deliver an event or workshop then break to eat a hearty lunch with my husband that has been cooked for us before sitting down for a long afternoon of writing. Dinner is a healthy meal (again, that I haven't cooked!) eaten together as a family. After getting the kids to bed, I read Richard Osman's fifteenth *Thursday Murder Club* book (I really, really hope you have them in you, Richard) or watch something silly on TV with my husband (Channel 4, please give us more *PhoneShop*), then go to sleep next to him without any night-wakings from our kids!

My Ideal Lifestyle: Living between London and Berkshire for most of the year, spending summers in New York (close to my family). Travelling at least twice a year with my husband and kids to new destinations, regularly conversing in a foreign language. Travelling locally and internationally for speaking engagements and events. Writing for large portions of each day while all of our home admin needs get taken care of by our 'home team'.

Ideal Legacy: Now, I'm not going to bare my entire soul here (ex-intel officers are legally bound to keep secrets!) but I'll share with you what I would be proudest of at the end of my life: knowing that I gave my one go-round this planet my best and bravest shot, and that I lived life as an adventure.

Now that you've gotten a glimpse of my Three Ideals, what might they be pointing to? Well, what's important to me is pretty obvious: family, travel, learning, engagement with the world, creativity and contribution. And what's not important to me is also obvious (sometimes by its absence): material stuff, household work, debt, admin in all its forms.

Similarly, when you do these exercises for yourself, there will be aspects of your Three Ideals that overlap and echo, so be attuned to the patterns, the repeats and the elements that ring deeply for you. When you look fully inward, these clues will start pointing towards whatever and wherever your personal Mission might be.

Then, the next step is to find ways to *live* your ideals so you can see what they feel like in reality (not just in the dreamscape of your mind) and whether living them might reveal yet more clues about your Mission.

The Cycle in Action: Processing and Analysis

To do that, to test and live your ideals, you need to process and analyze the data.

What *parts of your ideal day and ideal lifestyle resonate deepest and get you most excited?* These are the parts that I'd suggest you experiment with first. (Uncovering your Mission is all about experimentation and hypothesis.) For me, it was writing and speaking publicly, so those were the elements I wove into my day-to-day life first.

How *specifically are you going to live parts of your ideal day and ideal lifestyle?* For my ideals, I could have incorporated writing and speaking into my life in many ways but I started with a blog (something low-pressure and no-deadline that I could control) and by speaking at events that others had organized (bolting on to something existing instead of creating it from scratch meant that I had fewer hurdles to prevent me from starting).

When *are you going to live parts of your ideal day and ideal lifestyle?* This is not a broad temporal question – 'when I retire', 'when I've got more headspace', etc. – but a specific one. All of that work we did in Chapter 1 around doing, dumping and delegating means that you should have room in your life to experiment. So, when are you going to do the doing? Give me a day and a time, please. For example, I initially wrote my blogs on Wednesdays but now I do them every Sunday morning. I initially did speaking gigs once every few months, now I do them a few times a week.

Where are you going to live parts of your ideal day and ideal lifestyle? This was straightforward for me: writing happened in my home office; speaking happened at whichever venue the organizer chose. What about you? Where do you need to be or go to live parts of your ideals now?

And finally, *who do you need to bring on board or get involved so you can live parts of your ideal day and ideal lifestyle now?* For example, I initially had to identify and reach out to event organizers to pitch myself for speaking gigs; now I have a wonderful agent who does this for me.

Once you've processed and analyzed the intel, it's time to organize it in a usable way. At the Agency, this meant writing a finished intelligence (finintel) report that summed up the key messages and background information about the question being answered.

For our purposes, your finintel will summarize **what you think your Mission might be, or what the leads are pointing to, and how you are going to test this/incorporate it into your daily life.**

Your Mission

Based on my examples, my finintel report could have read something like:

'The patterns from my Backstory and Three Ideals suggest my Mission might be based around helping others . . . maybe something along the lines of writing and speaking about something I have an expertise in that others are interested in, too. Just thinking about this excites me, so it is a good place to start my experiment. I'm going to test what topics I feel called to write and speak about by starting a blog and speaking at events for entrepreneurs because I am already tapped into those networks and I know what it is like to be a founder. I'm going to create space in my life for this experiment by H-L-L-H'ing and 3D-ing as much as I can in my business and home life. I will talk to my husband about my plans – he always has great and practical ideas.'

The Cycle in Action: Dissemination

Once you've distilled your findings into coherent and actionable finintel, it's time to share that report with the people who need to know (NTK). Tread carefully here – not everyone in your life deserves access to your deepest intelligence. Keeping things on a NTK basis will require discrimination and judgement. Does your best friend make the cut? Maybe, maybe not. The members of your supporting Ops Team have to be carefully chosen and in the next chapter we'll see how sometimes the people closest to us can be the ones holding us back the most.

Executive Order: Putting the Intelligence Cycle to work may feel a bit messy and intense, but stick with it. Have fun with it. And carry the weight of it lightly. Finding and living your Mission doesn't have to mean anything more or less than what you want it to mean.

Your Mission can be to save the polar ice caps or it can be to save your sanity by making cold pressed juices. It can be to make Mars habitable by starting a space exploration company or it can be to make your body more habitable by sticking to a health routine. It can be to create staggeringly beautiful poetry that lasts through the ages or it can be to write staggeringly mediocre poetry that lasts until you throw it into the garbage (and who are any of us to decide what is beautiful or mediocre anyway?).

It doesn't have to be a Big Thing, this Mission of yours. It just has to be meaningful to you, to how you want to live and how you want to show up each day. Because you only get to be on this planet, to live this life, to be who you are once. Just one single solitary once.

So like I said, have fun with it, carry the weight of it lightly and just go with whatever Mission speaks to you the most.

Your Mission Motto

To help balance the weight with the lightness, the importance with the irrelevance, the open exploration with the defined personalization, I encourage you to think about a Mission Motto that captures the main essence of your ideal legacy.

My Mission Motto has always been 'never say no to an adventure'. This motto has helped me stay upright on the wobbly balance beam of life each time I've, well, wobbled. It helped me choose performing in the Opening and Closing Ceremonies of the London 2012 Olympics instead of getting an CV-enhancing internship during the summer between my first and second years as an MBA student. It helped me choose starting a business over getting a 'real job'. It helped me choose becoming a parent (twice!) instead of staying happily childless. And it helped me navigate all manner of big and small forks in the road. Sure, getting an internship, or a real job, or not having kids would have created adventures of a different kind but I already knew (broadly, anyway) what those adventures felt like and I wanted to push myself into new ones.

This Mission Motto of mine reminds me what is important to me, in the moment and in the final moments. It reminds me what I want to fill my life with. And what I want to fill my stories with when I'm 100 years old and telling anyone who will listen what it was like to be alive on this marvellous planet this one time I was given the gift to move around it.

Note that I said 'adventure', not fun. Because fun is fleeting and superficial but adventure can be eternal and deep. I can suffer during an adventure and still find it thrilling. I can fall during an adventure and still find it worth standing back up. I can go on inner adventures (the scariest and most exhilarating kind) and outer ones. Big adventures and small ones. Daily ones and lifelong ones. My marriage is an adventure. My non-linear career is an adventure. My Mission is an adventure. My inner growth is an adventure. All of these things are adventures – I choose to see them as adventures – and I never say no when I find the next one. I want the rollercoaster highs and the vomit from the plummets. I want the feels. I want the aliveness. And I want the, well, adventure.

So what is your Mission Motto? If you had to condense your ideal legacy into a phrase or two, what would it be? What is guiding your decisions now and what do you want to guide your decisions from now on?

As with everything we've done, your motto has to be yours and important to you. Nothing else.

This is your one go-round on this planet after all. What, at its core, do you want that to mean?

Key Intel

- Finding your Mission (the thing that gives life to your life) will require experimentation and reflection.
- The Intelligence Cycle framework can help you process and analyze the themes and patterns that emerge from your Backstory, your Three Ideals and all the work we've done together so far so you can then start to experiment with *living* your ideals and seeing what additional leads and ideas are generated when you do.
- If you're struggling to identify a Mission, start with being fully alive and actively engaged in your life instead of passively trudging along – the aliveness will open your eyes to new ideas, opportunities and connections and you can act on those.
- Your Mission Motto will help you navigate the many big and small decisions you'll have to make over a life-time and remind you that you can live and build your ideal legacy now.

Chapter 4
Your Ops Plan

Case File – Choosing an Ops Team

Back when I was starting my first business, I remember being haunted by a phrase that a friend had shared with me: *'You are the average of the five people you spend the most time with.'* And when I did an inventory, I didn't like what I found.

When I was at the CIA, the people around me, my team, were everything. I worked with and had access to specialists and experts of every imaginable function and capability (and many functions and capabilities that would stretch the limits of most imaginations). So when I left the CIA and all those doers and thinkers and brilliant odd-balls behind, it took a while to adjust to the MBA version of doers and thinkers and brilliant odd-balls, but it was a relatively smooth transition.

But when I started working for myself, by myself, I was isolated and on my own for most of each day, and when I was around other people, the five I saw the most were my husband, my mother-in-law (who I adore) and some very kind but going-nowhere friends.

You can see why the phrase about 'the five people' haunted me. Because, my husband aside, my five at the time weren't exactly a team of people that were going to propel me or challenge me or help me grow in any meaningful way.

And for almost a year I struggled along, intellectually and physically alone. And then one day, two of my favourite and most growth-oriented friendpreneurs and I started a WhatsApp group, a small move that proved to be one of the most life-enhancing and business-boosting decisions I've ever made. Our little threesome was – and still is – exactly what I needed to keep me and my business growing, improving and evolving, just as my CIA team and MBA colleagues had done before. The advice we share with each other has expanded our minds and our bank accounts, and the we've-got-your-back ethos of our group has staved off endless quagmires of frustration, confusion, anxiety and stuckness (being a founder isn't the hoodie-clad hootenanny pop culture tells us it is!). Our small size is the source of our might – we trust each other, know each other and are invested in each other, something that can get lost in bigger groups.

But not all WhatsApp groups or business groups or entrepreneur groups or groups of any kind are created equal, no matter their size. We have to go where the standards are high. Where the expectations are massive. Where we will rub elbows with people who don't make us feel desperate for a shower afterwards. As I had to do way back then, and as we'll be doing together in this chapter, the key is to select the best Ops Team for the mission at hand, the best people for where you're going and what you're about. Like that chalice in the Indiana Jones film, you have to *choose wisely* . . . or risk a desiccated death!

In any intelligence operation, the Ops Plan is the key that turns on-paper Mission musings into real-life realities, so don't rush through this part. Planning might not be something you have ever prided yourself on – I used to see myself as a free spirit who was on the 'non-plan plan' of life – but if you want to make things happen, you have to plan for how to do that, and then put that plan into motion.

It's not enough to say you want something (too many people wish their lives away: 'I wish I had a different job', 'I wish my partner were more engaged with the kids', 'I wish I could afford x, y, z', etc., etc., etc.) and leave it at that. If you truly want something, then you have to stop talking and start doing. And your Ops Plan will help you do exactly that. It will help you take stock of where you are, where you want to go and how specifically you can bridge any gaps between the two.

Together we'll be mapping your Mission by identifying the resources, assets, gaps and requirements for that Mission, and get you thinking through the contingency plans you'll need to put in place to see off the knowable problems/hurdles that can arise. We'll then interrogate the intel to make sure your plan is sharp and focused – and realistic! – and then work on pulling together that all-important Ops Team that will help you see your Mission through.

Mapping the Mission

Whenever we decide to make a change or do something important – especially something as personally resonant as a Mission – it can be tempting to go guns blazing into the sunset and do something dramatic and showy. But real life isn't Hollywood and the blazing guns are better swapped with detailed 'maps' that help you identify concretely what **resources and assets** you have available, what your **gaps** are and the **requirements** to fill those gaps. When you properly map your mission (or anything else you want to achieve), you make success infinitely more likely and blundering into hidden or obvious traps much less so.

Resources and assets

Mapping your Mission will require you to first take stock of your resources and assets. These are the **physical resources, people/interpersonal resources, knowledge resources,**

financial resources, time resources and energy resources you already have that can support your mission. Write them down, and be thorough and lateral.

Let's say you identified turning your side-hustle into a full-time, profitable business as your (potential) Mission. Maybe creativity and turning ideas into reality was something that came up again and again in your most fulfilled times and happiest memories from your Backstory. During your Intelligence Cycle exercise, you identified financial independence as the **'what'** of your Mission. Freedom over how and where you invest your time is also a theme that comes up in all of your Three Ideals; no offices or set-for-you routines are anywhere in sight.

To test this ideal and see if growing your business and becoming a full-time business owner might be your Mission (or lead you towards it), you might put together the list below of the resources and assets you already have available to you:

- **Physical resources:** Your business website and your existing product or service.

- **People/interpersonal resources:** Your customers and acquaintances you've met at meetup groups for part-time business owners. You also have a friend from school who has been running her own successful business for years and a former colleague who teaches business tutorials on YouTube.

- **Knowledge resources:** You're good at the creative side of things and connecting with customers but a bit lean on the more technical aspects of business (raising investment, financial management, growing a team, etc.).

- **Financial resources:** You're a bit strapped for cash to invest into your business at the moment because your baby has just started at daycare and your savings are nil.

- **Time resources:** Never enough hours in the day! But with your baby in daycare, there are probably a few hours to play with between when your day job ends and when you pick her up.

- **Energy resources:** Below zero. Having a career and a kid *and* a side-hustle is exhausting!

Gaps

Now that you've specified the resources and assets that you *do* have, you'll also get a clear picture of what you don't have. These are your gaps, which you will need to write down. In the list above, knowledge, financial and energy resources are the main gaps. So now let's put together your . . .

Requirements

Your requirements are a checklist for **what** you need to do to fill the gaps identified and **how** you are going to fill them.

What you need to do on each of the gaps:

- **Knowledge resources gap:** Get smart on fundraising and money management to begin with; these are going to be essential to scale your business.

- **Financial resources gap:** Come up with a budget for/ project the likely costs for your business growth plans so you can then look to fundraise.

- **Energy resources gap:** Gotta find a way to juice up those batteries, especially with your little one waking up so many times in the night.

And now the fun part where you get to come up with creative solutions about **how** to fill the identified gaps:

- **Knowledge resources gap:** You've contacted your local chamber of commerce/business hub to see what free courses and resources might be available to you. You're also starting to read business books and magazines, as well as tuning into your former colleague's YouTube channel, to learn how other founders went from being bossed to being the boss.

- **Financial resources gap:** You've involved your partner in your Mission exploration and have come up with a joint savings plan to squirrel away money that you can put towards growing your business. In addition, you've both agreed to take the bus to work twice a week (it takes longer but is cheaper than driving and paying for parking ... and as you learned from your H-L-L-H quadrant exercise, you can bolt on something you love – reading a book – to something you don't love – commuting to work on the bus; see how combining the layers we've laid down lets you eat cake!). You've also decided to cut out one oat-milk latte each week, cancel the gym membership you never use and bring lunch from home instead of buying it at work each day. (Damn, look at you go!) These savings will allow you to hire one part-time assistant immediately so you can take on more clients/customers while still working full-time in your day job.

- **Energy resources gap:** In the short term, you've asked your partner to come home early and be on 'night duty' two days a week so you can invest that time in building your business and going to those free business classes you found. (In the medium term, you may also want to look at nutrition, stress, hormones and anything else that can help/hurt your energy levels.)

Wow, you badass, you! You've just taken an amorphous thing like an 'ideal' and a 'Mission' and made it into a concrete reality by thinking it through, mapping it out in detail, and using those creative mind muscles of yours to make it happen. Where once there was never enough time or money or energy or even a clue about what would rev up your life (or side-hustle), now you are making things happen like a boss. Rock on.

Contingency Planning

Let's keep you in your everything-is-possible freewheel and find more creative solutions to the problems that might get in the way of your Mission. Because, let's face it, all plans need contingencies. Partners sometimes have to stay late at work or get stuck in traffic, babies get sick and want no one else but you and those freebie business classes you were once excited about turn out to be slow and basic.

Stuff happens.

But that doesn't mean it has to catch you with your pants down. Most problems can be foreseen with a bit of forethought. That's what good contingency planning is all about. It's a three-step process in which:

1) You list the **most likely** and the **most disruptive** potential problems.
2) Come up with a **plan or solution** to address each one.
3) Put the **contingency** into place.

Sticking with our scenario above, the contingency planning steps could look something like:

Example one:

1. My partner sometimes has to work late unexpectedly (potential problem).
2. If this happens on a growing-my-business night, I can have Mom on standby to watch our baby (solution).
3. I will call Mom right now and ask her if she can keep Tuesday evenings free in case we need her for baby cover (putting the contingency into place).

Example two:

1. Our baby sometimes has nights where she won't settle unless I'm the one doing the settling (potential problem).
2. I'll settle her as quickly as I can but if I'm tired the next day and need to catch up on sleep then I'll do more business-related work on Saturday (solution).
3. I'll do some searching to see if/when there are any weekend classes or Zoom sessions for the business fundamentals I'm brushing up on. If there are, great, I'll sign up for those (putting the contingency into place). If not, I'll repeat steps 2 and 3 until a viable solution is found and actioned.

Example three:

1. The free business classes I've signed up for might end up sucking (potential problem).
2. If that happens, I'll enrol in free classes led by professors from top-tier business schools (solution).
3. I've done some research and it looks like there are lots of free and highly rated mini-courses I can sign up for so I've saved them in my browser's bookmarks. I've also applied for a small business grant that I can use to fund some non-free courses . . . or maybe even a part-time MBA (putting the contingency into place).

We could do endless iterations of what could go wrong and how to address it but I think by now you get how this all works. It's pretty straightforward and can create powerful results and change you never dreamed possible. But you need to invest time in thinking and planning.

Most of us don't think about our lives in any structured, analytical way – I've said that before, I know, but funda-mental truths bear repeating – so start getting used to this new, thoughtful way of living and leading. That's why you're on this ride with me, after all, and that's how you can be a bit more CIA every day.

Interrogating the Intel

Speaking of being more CIA, no Ops Plan would be complete without a final interrogation of the intel and all of the relevant information you've collected for your Mission and your Ops Plan so far. This means identifying and interrogating all of the **underlying assumptions** in your plan ('Will my partner really be able to come home early twice a week?') and **stress testing** it against your real life ('Oh shoot, she will be out of the country for that conference in the spring . . . and again for that leadership retreat in the summer').

Everything is infinitely possible – definitely. BUT everything is not infinitely possible at the same time. Trade-offs are real. And interrogating the data will help you identify – and then come to terms with – the trade-offs you need to make.

We all have only so much time, energy and resources at hand, and each minute, unit of energy and utilized resource put towards one thing means it can't be utilised towards another thing. Each hour that I am fully engaged with my daughters in play and connection is an hour I am not being engaged in my work. Each exertion I make at the gym is an exertion I can't make at my desk. That's not good or bad; it's just a trade-off.

Most people are not willing to admit trade-offs exist, much less accept them consciously. But you are not most people. (Not after all the work we've done together!) So **interrogate** what your Mission is adding to your life and also acknowledge what it might need you to say no to. For example, I am very aware that sometimes my writing and my speaking will take me physically away from my family but that is a trade-off I am willing to make when it's important.

And you have that choice, too. Live your Mission, please. But remember that every time you say yes to it, you have to say no to something else. And that is OK. That is how it works. And the people who are impacted by your 'no's' will understand (hopefully) if you give them the chance to. (And if they don't, more on your Ops Team coming below.)

While writing this book, for example, my heart would lurch every time my daughter asked me to play with her because I needed to say no and focus on writing. After agonizing over how to shield her from my work, I decided to explain it to her. I sat her on my lap, told her that I am writing a book, explained how important it is to me, and that I will only be working on it for a defined amount of time, so can she please play without me for now? Soon after that conversation, I overheard her telling my husband, 'Daddy, Mommy can't play right now because she has to write her book down.' (I definitely cried at that one.) Instead of pushing her away, I invited her into my Mission and made the trade-off less painful. She then processed my writing time/being unable to play with her on her terms. And it took the bite out of the trade-off I was making for her, too.

So interrogate the data. Stress-test your mission. Own the trade-offs that are required . . . And let the people in your life pleasantly surprise you.

Executive Order: I want to take a pause here because your Ops Plan is where intangible theory meets hard reality. And for almost everyone, the hardness of the reality often comes from a lack of time, energy or financial resources.

Now, if you're H-L-L-H'ing and 3D'ing as you should, time will be less of an issue (and it only gets better with practice!). And if you're tuning into and working in alignment with your PEM, energy will be in greater supply now too. But the main biggie we haven't delved into yet is your financial resources, so let's start to get those sorted now. Because a lack of financial resources is often blamed for operational failure-to-launch but sometimes (maybe a lot of times), behind seeming financial scarcity is a misalignment of priorities and not necessarily a lack of funds.

So my executive order for you is this: be thoughtful and honest about how and where you spend versus invest your money and – no surprise here – be structured and analytical about it.

Very roughly speaking, I tend to define 'spending' as something that brings fleeting joy/immediate pleasure, the (usually) small and frequent expenses that don't add lasting value to our lives or relationships: that coffee and bagel you always pick up on the way to work, the shoes you see on Instagram and buy on a whim, the frequent date nights at expensive restaurants, the credit card debt you rack up buying things to cheer you up when you are sad.

'Investing', on the other hand, I define as something that brings long-term joy/delayed gratification, the larger sums that go towards things that do add lasting value to our lives or relationships: the money for that conference that taught you how to scale your business, the therapy sessions with your partner that are helping you stay committed to each other, the daycare fees that will enable you to go back to work at a job that invigorates you . . .

And – you can probably see where I'm going here – to *invest* in your Mission, sometimes you'll have to stop *spending* on your indulgences (at least some of them, or at least for a certain period of time). To help you do this in a non-judgey, still-enjoy-life way, I've created a bonus cash flow worksheet that you can find at www.ciatoceo.com/bonuses to help you explore where you might be able to free up the financial resources you need to invest in your Mission.

And if you want a shortcut, the next time you are debating whether a purchase is an expense or an investment, think about it this way: investing your money will help you build *your* dream career/business/ life/Mission and spending your money will help you build somebody else's.

Choosing Your Ops Team

Now that you've mapped your Mission in detail and freed up resources to support it, the final link is to pull together your supporting Ops Team. These are the heroes and she-roes who will help, guide, propel and inspire you along your way. Your team can be made up of colleagues in the office, people in your industry, smart friends and every conceivable mix of human beings who are part of your world or once lived in this world.

The key criteria for selection is that you choose your operatives carefully based on their **skills** and whether they have **relevant experience** for the Mission at hand. And it's also important that you don't blindly put friends and loved ones on your team if they have no practical reason for being there.

Here's why.

After I graduated from business school, my sister and brother staged what I can only call an intervention. I was a newly minted MBA and they were worried (terrified) for me that by starting my own business I was carelessly tossing my life, my career and my MBA into the rubbish heap. 'Get a big name on your resume,' they implored, 'and then you can do your own thing.'

Their one-way conversation lasted a few hours and, despite the delicious cocktails we were drinking, my mouth tasted like bile and regret. *What if they are right?* my mind wondered, even though my mouth kept insisting, 'I'm an adult, I know what I'm doing.'

What if I failed? What if my business didn't take off? What if I was throwing away the chance to work somewhere 'impressive'? What if one of the dozens of management consulting firms MBAs are supposed to want to work at never bestow their vaunted credentials onto my CV? What if I was being as reckless as they thought?

Everything my siblings said made sense, so why couldn't I just do what they said and be sensible? Why couldn't I just go out there and get a 'real' job?

I have a theory (actually, I have a lot of theories, as you know by now, but for our purposes here, I'll stick to one) and it goes something like this: the people who know us or love us are often the ones who make it hardest for us to do something different or make a big change or pursue our Mission. So often, they keep us in a time warp where the way they once 'knew' us is who we have to stay, and sometimes wanting us to stay that way is more for their benefit than for ours. They may just want us to keep playing a certain role so it doesn't upset the equilibrium established over years of knowing each other or so it doesn't challenge their own safety and comfort. Or they may just want us to do things a certain way because they are trying to protect us. They are worried we might fail or get upset or ruin ourselves, and their advice is meant to shield us from all of those things.

But you know what? No one can do that for us. No one can keep disappointment at bay for us. No one can read what is in our heart of hearts the way we can (now that we are paying attention). No one else can tell us what our Mission should be. And no one can tell us what is risky or what is not because we all have different definitions of risk. We have to listen to our intuition, to our gut, to our own ideas of what we want and who we are, because sometimes, maybe a lot of times, the people in our lives have their own agenda and we can't let them live our lives for us.

Did I ignore my siblings and tell them to shove it? Of course not. I listened to them, tortured myself about whether they were right and then I forged my own way. I made my contingency plans (see, I've done all the stuff I'm asking you to do!) and then I put my all into making a success of my business because I had no choice. I worked hard (before I learned how to work smart) and I got there. I replaced my post-MBA income through my new business and put every-one's worries – including my own – to bed, once and for all.

But it was really, really, really effing hard. Especially in the beginning when my own doubts and insecurities kept creeping in, it made every phone call with my family that much harder. I couldn't bear to talk to them for fear that one of them would tell me to 'keep an eye out' for jobs, contact a head-hunter or do my business as a side hobby while working for someone else. All of their concern and anxieties only amplified my own and it took every ounce of strength I could muster to nod and mmm-hmm and then tune them out.

Because the thing I learned is that the people who 'know' us and love us aren't always right. They don't always belong on the Ops Team. And if we listen to them too readily, they can keep us from being who we want to be, who we know we can be. We can take their concerns on board, sure, but that doesn't mean we let those concerns stop us from actualizing our Mission or our vision for our lives. We can do things our way. Protect ourselves our way. Address all of their (and our) concerns in our own way. And sometimes, just tune them out.

Not everyone is worth listening to, no matter how much they love us. Not everyone is qualified to have an opinion, no matter how long they've been in our lives (I don't ask my hairdresser for tax advice, even though I've known her twice as long as my accountant) or how smart they are (and I'd never let my accountant decide how I should style my hair, even though she is a brilliant human). Sometimes we have to beware of the people who 'know' us and love us because they can be the biggest roadblocks and a lot of the time they simply don't know what they're talking about when it comes to *our* Mission.

Making a big change, accomplishing a big goal, living a Mission is too important and too personal to let other people decide for us. And that's why our supporting Ops Team has to be chosen based on experience and expertise in where we are going and who we are becoming instead of where we once were and who we were before.

I share this with you because selecting your Ops Team for your Mission (which will mean some people *don't* get selected) will probably feel awkward and icky. And it will probably mean cutting some very important people out of perhaps a big part of your life. But it doesn't mean slashing and burning through your relationships – I didn't stop speaking to my family because they didn't want me to become an entrepreneur! It just means choosing the right team for the Mission at hand and creating **boundaries** with everyone else.

If your Mission is to be a thoughtful, values-driven CEO in an industry full of brash gregarious types then create an Ops Team of other leaders who have a track record of creating quiet and powerful results who you consult with or meet up with regularly. These leaders can be leaders you've never met (more on that below), in your industry or a different industry, young start-up founders or seasoned corporate leaders. And then limit your interactions with the loudmouths – if you have to interact at all – to annual conferences or once-in-a-while social events.

If your Mission is to be the next big fintech founder, then find and choose an Ops Team of fellow founders, other founders in fintech, business experts, tech experts and talk to *them* about your business (they have the skills and relevant experience, after all). And limit conversations with your extended family to your kids' antics at school, Uncle Shekhar's diabetes, plans for this year's Diwali celebrations or what you're watching on Disney+ these days.

If your Mission is to sing in a choir, then create an Ops Team of other singers, choir-leaders, creatives and talk to *them* about your Mission, and limit conversations with your existing circle of friends to plans for the weekend, books you're reading and other 'safe' subjects that have nothing to do with your Mission.

In choosing your Ops Team for your Mission, you will inevitably find that you've simply grown out of some relationships and that is OK too. It is part of the process. It is simply a part of life.

I stopped spending time with any number of acquaintances over the years, not because they are bad or uninteresting people but because I have met so many people while pursuing my Mission who I relate to on far more levels. And – here are those trade-offs again – given how few the hours I have to spare, I'd rather invest that time in building relationships and having fun with people who get me as I am now and who keep me growing, evolving and expanding than spending it with people from my past who I feel I should keep in my life simply because they were once a part of it.

Because there is no stasis. There is only forward motion or reverse. Fulfilment or frustration. Growth or shrinkage. And the communities we are part of, the five people we spend the most time with – our Ops Team – will move us in one direction or the other, even if the movement is imperceptible. And that's why it's so important that we join groups and build teams where our ambitions and boldness are the norm; communities where we are accepted, under-stood and challenged, and networks that allow us to remain undiluted and undiminished against the voices that tell us what we 'should' do, 'should' want and 'should' be.

This is why it's so important that we choose our Ops Team wisely and give the rest of the world less of our time and consideration.

The communities, the people, the ideas that comprise your Ops Team don't have to be physical and you don't have to communicate with them directly. They can be made up of the authors you read, the podcasters you listen to, the thought leaders you follow, the online forums you join. All of the ideas and thoughts and conversations and inputs you imbibe are part of your Ops Team because they contribute to who you are and who you become.

I'm not talking about living in a bubble, creating an echo chamber or searching out information that confirms what you already know. I'm talking about surrounding yourself with ideas, people, conversations and any other inputs that elevate, stimulate and inform instead of ones that deflate, subdue or deform. As any computer programmer or nutritionist will tell you, garbage in = garbage out. And when you are pursuing a Mission important to you, you can't afford to give garbage a look in.

So *choose* what goes in, who you let in and how often you let them in, and don't sabotage your ops by letting nay-saying backstabbers – or well-meaning ignoramuses – onto the team.

You and your Mission need and deserve more than that.

Key Intel

- To make your Mission a concrete reality you will have to come up with an Ops Plan that maps out the resources and assets, gaps and requirements for your Mission and puts in place contingencies for when things go awry.
- Your contingency plan will require you to list the most likely and the most disruptive potential problems and come up with a solution to address each one.
- Stress test your Ops Plan by interrogating the intel and assumptions underpinning it; acknowledge and then accept the trade-offs that are required.
- To fund your Mission, think about where you are spending versus investing your financial resources and try to shift the balance towards investing.

Your Ops Plan

- Select the people on your Ops Team for their skills and relevant experience. People who have always been in your life won't always meet these criteria but you don't need to ditch them, just create boundaries around what you share and do with them.

Part One After-Action Review

We've been on a wild ride so far, dear reader, and I'm really pleased that you've started to give focused attention to big, tough questions because I know the transformative power that comes from grappling with them.

Everything is possible and you now have the structured, analytical toolkit to make it so for yourself. I am not going to come to your house to check that you've done your Backstory exercise or grade you on how detailed your Three Ideals are, or ask your employees if you've made PEM-based tweaks to your work schedule or allowed them to do the same. What I am going to do is assume that you care enough about making the most of your life to invest the time in working through what I've shared, and then put all the elements into action. One bit at a time.

With your new-found clarity about where you want to go, who you want to be and what you want to have – all the Thinking Bigger you've done – take a pause and conduct your own after-action review before moving on. Tinker, tweak, refine and reflect. Because in Part Two, we'll be leveraging your Part One toolkit to get you Leading Better by 'bossing' your life and becoming an even more powerful leader-by-example for yourself and others.

Part Two
Leading Better

Chapter 5

Part Two

Leading Better

Chapter 5
CO-yeS You Are

Case File: Redefining Leadership

Chiefs of Station (COSs) are the CIA bosses who run missions overseas. When I was serving in a war zone, I served under a COS who broke all stereotypes of what a COS was 'supposed to' be. Adam (not his real name) was a dream to work with. He understood the value that analysts brought to the intelligence party and was always supportive of my doing whatever needed doing to fill the requirements and gaps I was asked to fill by my team at HQ. We interacted as equals even though I was awed by his reputation and operational badassery. He treated me – and everyone else he worked with – like the integral parts of the mission that we were (well, some were more integral than others, but that didn't seem to change the way Adam treated anyone).

He called me 'sister'. He gave me use of his plane and his security team. He asked me what I needed and then helped me get it. He led without shouting, without bravado, without having to display how tough he was – all that alpha nonsense that erroneously gets conflated with being a 'boss', especially in the hyper-macho world of the CIA – and was the first to make it onto my great Agency leaders list.

Charles (again, not his real name) was another Great. He was a former Marine who made silly dad jokes, left poetry on our chairs and whose genuine kindness was only surpassed by his analytical prowess. He was who he was and took ultimate responsibility, even for things he couldn't control or wasn't responsible for. He didn't browbeat others into submission, like many of the shaky egos around him; he led by example. And to this day, I am deeply dazzled by his easy way of being both big-hearted and big-brained without needing to big-up himself.

And the final Great was Samantha (you know that's not her real name either). She was as tough-love as you get and made me want to meet her high expectations because I was inspired by what she saw in me and I wanted to prove her right. She also had a subtle finesse that dispatched the less-than-capable without them realizing she was doing so. She had no patience for slackers or rest-on-their-laurels career-ists, even among her 'superiors'. She played the political games required but kept herself and her integrity always solidly intact.

Adam, Charles, Samantha – they were great leaders but they also looked to me as a leader. And in doing so, they showed me that leadership has nothing to do with your title or the size of your office and everything to do with who you are, how you carry your identity and the size of your commitment. The reason they treated me as a leader was because I got shit done. I did things that needed doing without being asked. I came up with solutions to problems no one asked me to solve. I was great at what I did but never shied away from getting greater. Feedback was my friend.

Without back-slapping or fist-pumping or grandstanding, my Greats brought out the greatness in me. They showed me what leadership looks like and taught me to see and nurture it in myself. Without ego or defensiveness or shrinking from hard truths. And the same is true for you. You are already a leader and have the capacity to become a greater one. But you have to be prepared to shed the ego and defensiveness and accept hard truths. I'll show you how to do just that and together we'll redefine tired old notions of what leadership looks like so that you can start to see that it looks like you, too.

Being a leader in the field is more art than science and the best COS 'artists' I've seen are the ones who are so solid in themselves that doing the mental gymnastics required by their roles and bringing out show-stopping performances from others seems effortless.

But all good art takes work to look effortless. And everything you've done so far is going to go a long way towards helping you fully embody the kind of leader you already are and become an even better one. Leveraging the insights you uncovered in part one, we'll be looking at how Identity-Driven Leadership™ (IDL) can get you bossing it at work, at home, in your relationships and with yourself. We'll further channel your inner COS by building your confidence to see off 'terrorists' and help you R.E.S.E.T. behaviours that might be holding you or your Mission back.

Identity-Driven Leadership (IDL)

The best leaders I've worked with know who they are and don't try to be otherwise, while still allowing for improvement. For you, Identity-Driven Leadership will require exactly that: owning who you are (repercussions and all) and getting better in the areas where you might be letting yourself down, whether that's in how you live your values (or not) or how you deal with worry and stress and steer your teams through challenges. As you embrace your own way of leading – instead of contorting yourself into someone else's – you'll find you inevitably become a powerful example for others.

You won't be using your personas or profiles (or any of that work we did in Part One) as a sledgehammer to browbeat others into your-way-or-the-highway dictatorship but you will start to integrate what you've discovered about yourself in all areas of your life, like any good field agent and COS would.

Owning Who You Are

Part of embodying your IDL style is to admit that you have standards and expectations and preferences for how you want things done. It doesn't matter if someone else thinks they are stupid or over the top or irrelevant because no one else can tell you what you care about. And that's why it's so important in business (and in life) to accept what goes with your IDL territory and ask for what you want.

When I stopped shying away from who I am and started asking for what I wanted, it made life easier for everyone. I've asked assistants to use specific fonts in the presentations they put together for me, or to give me information in bullet points instead of block text. I've asked clients to agree to certain 'rules of engagement' (show up on time, prepare in a certain way before our meetings, etc.) so they can get the best out of me and the most from our time together. And at home, I've asked my partner to cook a certain recipe for dinner or to take the kids out of the house for a few hours because I needed quiet time. I ask nicely, of course, but am very specific. Does this make me a diva, or just decisive?

Because the way I see it, it's far better to be clear about what we expect or want from others instead of being passive-aggressive about it. If something is important enough for us to care about, then we should make a point to communicate it. This is just an easier way to live. You wouldn't go to a new restaurant and expect the waiter to intuit what you wanted so why expect your partner/clients/suppliers/colleagues to do so when the stakes are even higher?

Just communicate what you want, exactly how you want it and take the guesswork out of it. And be specific as to which instructions are must-haves and which can be executed within general parameters. It doesn't mean you'll always get what you want but at least it leaves no room for misinterpretation. And then any results that are other than what you've asked for are failures of execution, not failures of communication (assuming you've given good, clear instructions and then gotten out of the way!).

Leading is about taking responsibility. When you communicate what you want specifically you are accepting ultimate responsibility and freeing the people in your life from the stress of not knowing or unwittingly under-performing (wilful under-performing is a totally different matter). Clear, precise instructions set the recipient up to succeed, not fail.

So if you care about something, if you want something, if you have a certain way of doing things, a certain standard you want to adhere to, don't be embarrassed or act as if you don't. Own who you are and ask for it.

If you want your co-founder to do more of the tedious admin that has ended up on your desk, ask them to do more . . . and be specific about what they need to take lead on. If you want your partner to do more at home so you have time to build your business, ask them to do more . . . and be specific about your new division of labour. If you want your bookkeeper to send you your P&L statements each month so you can review them during your Golden Hours, ask them to do it . . . and be specific about what information you want them to highlight. If you want something but aren't sure whether it exists, ask Google if it does. Ask, ask, ask and ask again, and be specific. Your SA-ing and PEM-ing in Part One will have helped you understand your needs and wants more concretely, so be concrete when you share your needs with others!

The more you ask, the more you'll get (life is a numbers game) and the more you'll see that being a good leader or CEO or partner or parent isn't about testing other people to read your mind, it's about giving them the tools and instructions to succeed without having to do so.

Executive Order: We're not often encouraged to be straight with people. Even though our daily lives are not the stuff of spy thrillers, we treat human interactions as an endless game of guile and ciphers and mysteries and riddles. So I'm here to order you to practise being more candid. You don't have to be a dick about it – it's not my-way-or-the-highway – but you can be clear. Frame it to the people around you as an insight into how you operate and an invitation for them to share the same with you. I'll show you mine, as it were, and you can show me yours.

As I've started to communicate my expectations and needs and standards to others more openly and consistently, everyone around me has benefitted because they no longer have to guess or tip-toe and wonder if they'll hit a minefield. There are no minefields because I've given them the map. They know what I expect, and in turn, I tell them what they can expect from me.

So be real and honest with the people around you – again, in a non-dick way – and invite them to get real and honest with you. Neither side has to like what they hear or has to conform, by the way, but everyone can use the knowledge that is shared to make an informed decision about how, or if, to proceed in the relationship.

Living Your Values

While you are getting real with yourself and others about your specific needs and wants, let's take it a bit deeper and get real about your bigger-picture needs and wants, i.e. your values. Because to be a leader in any meaningful way – even if 'just' a leader of your own life – you have to show up for what's important to you and make sure the integrity chain between what you value and what you do remains un-chinked.

When I was at the CIA, one of our core values was 'speaking truth to power'. This wasn't just a nicety plastered on the walls, this was something we all were called on to live each day, in big and small ways. Sometimes that meant pushing back against a supervisor's opinion; sometimes that meant telling the President of the United States that a specific policy wasn't working; and sometimes it meant telling a general when he was being blindsided by the wrong metrics. We didn't drop truth bombs and walk away. We backed up our truths with the power of proof.

It was uncomfortable and awkward and sometimes terrifying, but there was a strong culture of being honest, of 'knowing the truth and letting the truth make you free', even when that truth hurt. Sure, there were times when we did this imperfectly or messily, but we did it. And that's how it is for our personal values, too. We have to live them for them to count as being ours. Mess and all.

If we say we value family but spend our whole day working (even if it's work we enjoy and care about), only showing up for bedtimes and mealtimes while still welded to our phones, that's not living our values. We don't get to claim that one.

If we say we value our health but eat whatever pre-wrapped garbage is easiest to swallow because we're so busy with other things that we can't prepare (or order!) actual food, that's not living our values. We don't get to claim that one.

If we say we value integrity but cut corners or do things half-assed because we can't be bothered to give it our all, that's not living our values. We don't get to claim that one.

And if we say we value ourselves but don't look after our health, don't go to the doctor about that niggling thing, don't invest in ourselves, don't stand up for ourselves and don't tell that inner voice in our heads to shut up whenever it's being a bastard about how we look or how we perform, that's not living our values either. We don't get to claim that one.

We don't get to say we value family, health, integrity, ourselves and then live differently. That's not how it works. Either we're honest about how we are living and say we really value work, junk food, expedience and being shitty to ourselves OR we change our behaviour and get to claim the values that we want to (family, health, integrity, ourselves).

Too often we overcomplicate intangibles like values but if we say we care about something, then we have to show that tangibly in what we do and how we show up every day. It is as simple as that.

So as you start to emerge from your leadership chrysalis, take stock of your values. Go through your Backstory, your Mission, all that good internal stuff you've started to externalize, and tune in. Identify what you are telling yourself you care about (for me it is family, contribution, creativity and curiosity – these values are so important to me they made it into my marriage vows) and then compare that list with how you are living your life each day. Where is there alignment? Where is there a disconnect? Once you've identified where you are and aren't living your values, you can bridge any gaps by creating an Ops Plan, or simply by doing what it is you say you value and showing up more often – ideally always – for the things you say you care about.

I had a harsh reckoning a few years ago when I realized I was only exercising once a week on average yet I kept telling myself I value good health. What a hypocrite! So I got my habits in line, started to eat real food again – stuff made from plants, not made in a plant! – got to the gym more regularly and tracked my stats so I couldn't fool myself about how much I was or wasn't exercising. It was only after I realigned my values with my actions that I got to claim the 'good health' value back (the alternative was to claim 'bad health' as something I value because that's how I was behaving, but that option was a non-starter).

So check yourself. And then correct yourself. IDL is about being your whole self and you can't be whole if you are full of holes when it comes to living your values.

Dealing with worry and stress

Being whole, being clear and specific with ourselves and with others about who we are and how we operate can be terrifying, stressful and uncomfortable. Some of us – maybe all of us – will bring to mind all manner of disasters, confrontations and upheaval that will ensue from living more thoughtfully and in line with who we are. But instead of letting our worst-case hamster spin the wheels of our minds into a frenzy, we can boss that little rodent into submission by doing what all Agency officers do: **rehearse the disasters**.

Before I deployed to a war zone, I had to undergo weeks of training that prepared me for all manner of terrifying scenarios: coming under heavy fire, getting kidnapped, being in a car chase, triaging lethal wounds. I had to rehearse these scenarios so my instructors and I could see how I would respond and then they could help me work through any deer-in-headlights instincts.

I remember vividly an exercise we carried out in the dead of night. I was stopped at a checkpoint by gun-wielding 'terrorists'. There were no blockades, no barriers, nothing other than two men in keffiyehs shouting at me and waving rifles in the air. Me in the driver's seat, my instructor sitting next to me and my fully functional car purring under me. And what did I do? I pulled up to the checkpoint and froze. The mock-terrorists screamed at me. They opened my car door. They reached in and put my car in park and I still didn't move. They took my seatbelt off of me, pulled me out of my seat and slammed me against the car, still frozen. Click. 'You're dead,' one of them said in my ear. And then he let me slink back into my car.

If I had been in the field, I would have been kidnapped or killed. The distance between staying alive versus ending up in terrorist clutches was the two inches between brake pedal and accelerator. My car was in gear but my brain was not. (I had gone 'black' in SA terms.) That lesson will never leave me. And that's why it's so powerful to rehearse the disasters you are anxious about because you get to test how you will respond when the stakes are negligible and do better when things get real.

Say you are dreading talking to your co-founder about what specifically you need from him so you can operate at your best and grow your company. He has been free-riding on your hard work and you need him to step up in certain areas so you can both see your business through its next big transition. BUT being honest about what you need and how you want things to change elicits, well . . . at first, it elicits nothing but vague anxieties about upsetting the status quo and the hellish can of worms that will open. So you rehearse the disasters.

You imagine the upturned tables and smashed computers you think your co-founder will leave in his wake as he storms out in a blaze of fury and shouts you down for questioning his commitment. In your mind, you counter his shouting by listening. You meet his denials with data. You think about what you will say once he's had his say. You plan for a follow-on call or meeting once he's calmed down. You present your case as a business case, not a personal one and ask him for ideas and solutions to the perceived problem.

You brace yourself for the possibility that he might quit. Or demand that you quit. And you rehearse that disaster, too. What happens if one of you has to go? If you were to buy him out you'd have to do X, Y, Z but it will be better in the long run because of A, B, C. Or if he buys you out, you'd get X amount of money and be able to do Y with it.

For each disaster you imagine, each anxious outcome you envision, each potential problem, you come up with a plan, a solution, an action that you can take. And you make peace with all of the potential eventualities – even though you're not sure which one will materialize – because you now know how you might handle each one. You've played all of the disasters out to the end and rehearsed them into submission. And slowly, slowly, the anxiety that was once an amorphous blob fogging up your head, thumping through your every waking hour and sapping your lifeforce, is now given the attention it deserves. That is to say: none. Because now you see that all of the scenarios that scared you are not actually that scary after all. The dread you had conjured up has been replaced with a clear-eyed pairing of potential disaster with potential solution, and you have shown yourself that even if the worst were to happen you could handle it. And you would move forward.

And damn, look how you've bossed your worries! You now realize that all you had to do – all you ever have to do when you are faced with big or small anxieties or stresses – is give the amorphous disaster a concrete form and rehearse what you would do in the face of each one. And then refocus all the time and energy you were previously pouring into worrying into finding solutions and planning actions that will mitigate the disastrousness of each specific scenario. Bad. Ass. Boss.

And then in real life, you have the tough conversation with your co-founder. And things get better or they don't. But you're not worried about it because you know what you'll do in any of the scenarios that previously scared you most.

Worry and stress will always be lurking. But instead of cowering in a corner, eyes closed and frozen in place – instead of going 'black' – you took back control. You led yourself, and those around you, through an anxious time by working through potential disasters from every angle and rehearsing them until all you were left with was a list of tangible actions you could take to address them. You shoved that worry and stress into the corner you once would have hidden in. Like I said: Bad. Ass. Boss.

Each time you stop letting worry and stress consume you, each time you focus on what you can control and come up with solutions, each time you don't freeze in the face of terror, you'll gain a little more confidence with which to confront the next challenge, the next disaster. And then a little more. Because confidence isn't something you are allocated at birth and tough luck to anyone who got shafted. Confidence is something you develop by seeing yourself through inner and outer challenges. By doing hard things. By rehearsing the disasters and then handling them.

Hopefully you won't ever need to confront terrorists, real or otherwise, but now you know how to confront whatever terrorizes you and boss it into oblivion.

R.E.S.E.T.-ing Your Internal Ops

Your new-found rehearsal skills will come to more good use as you employ them to R.E.S.E.T. the behaviour patterns that don't serve you or your Mission.

For much of my life, I have been a very impatient person. I chalked this up to: A) being a New Yorker ('big city girls don't have time to waste!'); B) my father ('short fuses are in long supply in my DNA') or C) inevitability ('that's just who I am!'). Nothing to do with me as an active participant in my life, mind you, just something I was because that's how I was. But the problem was I didn't want to be impatient. It was exhausting being so easily irritated. It was a behaviour pattern I wanted to change.

So I did some digging and reflecting. And then I decided to do an experiment by asking two important questions: What if being impatient wasn't a fundamental flaw in my makeup but a well-worn habit? And if it was just a habit, could I swap it for a better one?

It was while I was mulling this over and experimenting with solutions that I came up with a way to R.E.S.E.T. my internal ops and get uncomfortable with the impatience that I was far too 'comfortable' with:

R – I **reviewed my rationalizations**. Was being impatient something inevitable like I always told myself it was or was it just a habit I had perfected through constant use? I chose to see it as the latter because I am the driver of my life, not a passenger, and as such, I could drive myself in a different, better direction if I wanted to. So then I decided to . . .

E – Find a **new exemplar**. What was the new behaviour I wanted to demonstrate? Well, I wanted to create a different paradigm for dealing with frustration. Instead of impatience, I wanted to exemplify patience.

S – So I **scenario-rehearsed** what the new exemplar behaviour would look like in the real world. I ran through scenarios involving customer service incompetence, slow-moving queues – slowness in all its forms! – triggering conversations with loved ones and all manner of potential irritants. And at the crucial point where I would normally start getting tetchy or defensive, I replaced that scene with one in which I took a deep breath (or ten), remembered what my end goal was (to get an issue resolved, buy my groceries, get to an appointment on time, maintain healthy relationships with my family, etc.) and proceeded with patience and calm.

E – Then, when I next found myself in an irritation-inducing scenario, I would **execute** the new behaviour I had rehearsed and **exercise** the new habit in real life.

T – And as I got executing and exercising, I made **tweaks** where needed (I found leaving the room when in a rising heat conversation with loved ones was a much better solution than staying and deep breathing, for example) and kept tweaking and tweaking until . . .

Hey presto! Impatience **R.E.S.E.T.** to patience.

Now, I know that might sound too easy and pat, but R.E.S.E.T.-ing behaviour patterns is anything but. It *is* simple but it is not easy. It takes practice and intention and awareness and experimentation and commitment. Sometimes I am text-book at keeping my cool and other times I am way, way less so. But I keep trying and keep getting a little bit better. And with enough practice and commitment, I know that being patient will become as reflexive as being impatient once was. But I have to keep at it. And so will you.

I'm not a psychologist or psychiatrist or anything that starts with *psych* and requires degrees and certifications, so this is not meant to be professional medical advice about behavioural issues that might require those things (I know you know this but my time at the CIA made me hyper aware about not assuming anything so I'm telling you outright!). What this is, is a tool you can use to at least try to take control of something that you may have once dismissed as uncontrollable (I genuinely believed that my DNA had stamped me with an impatience gene but DNA isn't destiny – and is there even a gene for impatience anyway?).

If we can control something – and behaviour is one of those things – then let's try to control it, R.E.S.E.T. it, boss it, even, instead of staying victim to the person we've told ourselves we inevitably 'are'.

Key Intel

- Identity-Driven Leadership is all about owning who you are, sharing that honestly with others, living your values and handling worry and stress like the badass leader you are.
- When you find yourself spiralling in anxiety or worry, rehearse all of the concrete (and relevant!) disasters you can imagine. Focus your energies on planning how you can mitigate/deal with each specific one.

- R.E.S.E.T.-ing your internal ops takes practice and commitment but you can change the behaviours that don't serve you; DNA is not destiny.
- You are the boss of your life and how you live it, not the other way around.

Chapter 6
War Games

Case file: Focusing on Your Mission

I grew up around a lot of Patel family wisdom. Between my two parents and the two sets of grandparents who lived with us, literally not a single day went by without some *kahevat*, or saying, being sagely passed down. Some were Gujarati classics (my favourite – *Khakhra ni khiskoli sakar no swaad su jaane?* – roughly translates into 'What would a squirrel who subsists on bland crackers know about appreciating sugar?' Or, more simply, some people have no taste! This one still comes up whenever we visit New York, by the way, because my dear English husband has been deemed the 'squirrel' who unfathomably can't appreciate the delights of Gujarati food) while other aphorisms were family originals.

I remember vividly a car ride to school one day when my dad said, in response to someone commenting longingly about a mansion we had just passed, that we should all try to 'live an absolute life, not a relative one'. And that bit of dad wisdom has stayed with me for decades.

So many of us don't seem to know where we 'are' or how we feel until we compare where that 'is' in relation to others. We feel good about our marriages because they are better than our friends' (but are we happy in them?). We are proud of our salaries because they are higher than our peers' (but are the 100-hour weeks worth it?). We get embroiled in all manner of materialistic brinkmanship because we want to have a nicer car/bigger house/more expensive clothes than those around us (but are we going into ruinous debt to fund these things?). We decide how we feel *after* we compare, without asking how we feel in our heart of hearts. We seek external signals for internal emotions.

We do this at school and at work, too. We don't decide if we are happy with our performance until someone praises us for it. We aren't proud of ourselves until someone gives us a gold star. (I once overheard a conversation where someone asked: 'If no one told you that you did a good job, how would you know that you did?' to which they got a response that quite literally blew my gold-star-hungry mind: 'I would just know.' Cue nuclear mushroom cloud and head-exploding emoji.)

Peeps, the need for external validation is a plague. Comparison might feel instinctive but, as we proved to ourselves in the last chapter, just because something feels like it is an inevitable part of who we are (or an inevitable part of the human condition), doesn't mean it has to be. We can choose *not* to live our lives with our heads on a swivel; I know because I made this choice. And this is the chapter where we're going to learn how, as my dad so powerfully put it, to live a more contented absolute life focusing on our Mission instead of a relentlessly relative one that focuses on everyone else's.

In life, as in the CIA, it's dangerous, distracting and destructive to focus on any mission but your own. In business, too much focus on competitors can drive us off course and turn our companies into poor facsimiles of someone else's. And whenever we do anything, especially anything as meaningful as our Missions, it can be tempting to fall – and a descent it is – victim to what I call comparisonitis. So in this chapter we'll be tackling ways to get you (re)focused on the things that are important to you without a sideways glance at what other people are doing.

We'll get your head back in the game when confronted with outer and inner critics, and go to war on mission creep – the near-constant pull many of us feel to do all the things. I'll arm you with tools that will help you regain laser-like focus whenever temptations and alluring distractions arise so that nothing and no one – not even yourself – can keep you from moving forward with your Mission.

Gear up and let's get going.

Comparisonitis: Public Enemy Number One

Many years ago, when I was in the early stages of one of my businesses, I remember having a particularly frenetic day where I was alternating between Zen-like focus and headless chicken frenzy. When I stopped myself to try to understand why I was being so manic, I realized the cause of my tailspin was that I had ignored one of my biggest rules: I had been comparing myself all day long to a close friend whose business had recently seen explosive growth. Now, normally thinking about this friend wouldn't affect me. He is gifted, generous, hard-working and deserves all of his success. But every now and then, my comparisonitis flares up and I have to force myself to liberally apply my father's antihistaminic aphorism: live an absolute life, not a relative one.

I get it. Being driven and ambitious and wanting to do big things – especially now that you've uncovered your Mission or are at least committed to doing so – inevitably pushes us all to strive and try as hard as we can. And in all that pushing and striving and trying, we start to look around – for inspiration, best practice, benchmarks, support, all that good stuff, sure – but sometimes, simply because comparison is what we are used to doing to measure ourselves. I know how that goes.

But the problem is that comparison is at best nominally illuminating and at worst totally deflating. Because how many of us would compare a child just learning to walk unfavourably against a world-class athlete like Jessica Ennis-Hill? It seems stupid to consider it. Yet that's exactly what we do when we compare our careers or our lives with someone else's. We judge ourselves today by where they are tomorrow. We get disheartened by our year one stats by comparing them to someone else's year ten. We look around and forget that we are seeing their outputs (or their highly curated social-media feeds), not their inputs. But we keep doing it anyway.

So whenever you find your comparisonitis coming on, here's how to scratch the itch without letting it become an all-consuming rash:

1) **Compare apples to apples.** Your year one, two or three will inevitably look different to someone else's year six, seven or eight. And even if you compare yourself at the same stage, their year one might still be meaningfully different to yours. (Are they in the same industry? Did you start with the same resources? Did you invest the same amount of money? Do you have the same competing pulls on your energies? Do you share the same number of non-Mission related responsibilities?) No two 'apples' are ever totally the same, so recognize where there are similarities but also appreciate the differences.

2) **Learn from what they have done.** Instead of being paralyzed by envy, try to dissect and analyze the more

successful businesses/people/relationships you see and try to understand how they got there. Read up on them, buy their biographies, listen to their podcasts, or – depending on who or what it is you are comparing yourself to – ask them directly. Once you know the 'how' you can apply and adapt the lessons that are relevant to you. Use your envy as a catalyst for learning and improving!

3) **Think about what you *have* accomplished.** Humans are notoriously lack-obsessed, so whenever you feel tugged at by comparison demons, force yourself to reflect on how far you *have* come, remind yourself how much you *have* grown. Compare yourself today with yourself just a few short months (or hours!) ago and acknowledge how much you have grown and/or changed for the better.

4) **Remember that everyone's path looks different.** We all have different pulls on our time, energy, emotions and capacity. And as a high-energy, 40-year-old mother of two who is close to her large, extended family, runs two businesses concurrently, advises other leaders and entrepreneurs and tries to keep fit and healthy while contributing to the world in different ways, my life and businesses inevitably look different and will evolve at different rates to the life and business of someone else who is single or younger or has different demands on their time. There are many paths to success and it's OK, inevitable even, for yours to look different to someone else's.

5) **Indulge in a micro-dose of something that makes you smile.** For me, that can be reading about NASA and the stars (our universe is wonderous beyond comprehension), watching *Jane the Virgin* (it is one of the funniest, most poignant and perfectly written shows I have ever seen), listening to my daughter sing 'How Far I'll Go' from *Moana* (it literally makes my heart feel like a Fourth of July fireworks display) or making a fresh stove-top coffee (the ritual of preparation is so satisfying). Indulging in small pleasures is a great pattern-break and smiling is the ultimate comparison reliever.

6) **Get it out there.** Talk to someone, write it down or have a chat with your Ops Team. Sometimes externalizing where you feel you are behind will show you where you aren't and will invite other people to give you their views and share their own experiences. We are the harshest judges of ourselves and talking to others or journaling our thoughts often helps us regain perspective. At the end of the day, no matter who you are or how 'high' you climb, there will always be people who are 'above' and 'below' you, people who have more and who have less than you, and people who are better and who are worse than you at something. That's life. And that is perspective.

It's not easy. Pursuing success as you define it, being who you are, focusing on your Mission – these are all fraught with demons and doubts and deflations. (Yes, even for people who seem to have it all together and appear totally at ease; you'd be amazed at how many leaders feel like they don't belong at the top.) But you are doing something – something big in its own way. In your own way.

Not all of us will head Fortune 500 companies or found unicorn businesses, not all of us will win industry awards or feature in business magazines and not all of us will live in McMansions or ever aspire to. And that's OK too. Of course it is.

But we will all achieve something bigger, be someone bigger, by running our *own* race to the top of wherever we choose to go.

Handling Inner and Outer Critics

(First, the outer ones . . .)

'Run your own race' is a lovely mantra and one that has helped many an Olympic athlete, CEO, inventor and pretty much any stripe of successful person stay focused on their Mission and not get side-tracked by other people's nonsense or noise. But sometimes that noise becomes unignorable because it takes a turn for the personal, the nasty or the threatening. Sometimes, even when we are safely siloed in our own hyper-focused Mission-centric bubbles, the hater-ade spewed at us burns through our forcefields like acid. Sometimes we are pulled into a battle with the kangaroo court of public opinion.

I know this from experience. I have had a number of outrageously ridiculous things happen to me. I've received stingingly nasty emails, sexually aggressive messages and threats to defile my professional reputation for the treasonous crime of – wait for it – inviting people in my network to a webinar. Yes, a webinar. This kind of thing happens way too often to women in particular when we step into the light, put our heads above the parapet and choose success, change and visibility over status-quo stagnation.

Hater-ade – and cruelty – flows through the veins of the internet. When we are pulled into that current, so often we are told to ignore it, laugh it off, 'lighten up' or 'learn how to take a joke'. But nothing about aggressive and attacking behaviour strikes me as humorous or comic. And when this kind of thing happens, it can destabilize and derail us from pushing forward with our success. However, we *can* challenge the notion that we should expect anonymous hatred if we are 'too' visible, 'too' attractive, 'too' famous, 'too' successful or 'too' anything. (It's that TM/NE problem I mentioned in Chapter 2 rearing its head again.) We can #OutThem or delete them or ignore them or anything in between. And we can do it with the support of the people around us, with our all-important Ops Team at our side.

When I got those hateful messages, I went straight to my small and mighty WhatsApp group of three, disoriented and shaken. My girl P.C. reminded me that getting haters is a sign that we are becoming bigger and better ('No one kicks a dead dog,' she sagely shared). And J.E. sent me some very poignant and funny videos from a vlogger who has received graphic hate posts and turned them into a powerful, insightful and witty conversation.

As we build our success, as our profiles grow, as we stretch and progress and make things happen, there will always, inevitably, be people who hate us because they are jealous, hate us because we are women/non-traditional/trans/non-white/non-alpha/gay/etc., or hate us simply because they are hateful. The world has always been this way. (And modern technology spews their venom further and faster.) But we are lucky to live in a world where we are not alone. Where we can rely on our Ops Team. Where we can turn to the same technology used by the assholes to find others who have experienced what we are going through and build strength in numbers. Where we can find our own ways to process what happens on our path to success. And continue to march on towards it.

Success will always breed haters. But as you become more successful, as you live more fully as yourself and in alignment with your values, and as you come into the crosshairs of the haters and trolls and naysayers of the world, whenever you are cut down, remember your Inner Steel persona and rise right back up.

Because what those people say or think about you is none of your business, and it has nothing to do with you. Their outsized and outrageous reactions to you being who you are and pursuing what you care about have everything to do with them and their need to project their self-loathing. You just happened to come along. It isn't personal. And it isn't unique to you. Haters are like pimples and taxes – unpleasant and unavoidable, but totally universal.

So keep staying your course, keep pursuing your Mission, keep being you and shine the fuck on. As the saying goes: success will be your best revenge.

(. . . and now the inner ones)

But sadly, sometimes your biggest hater will be you. Sometimes the most malicious voice you'll hear will be your own. And sometimes the person cutting you down the most ferociously is the one staring at you in the mirror. What did we do to deserve ourselves?!

Well, my friends, there are a few ways I've learned to keep my head in the game whenever I've battled myself, so here's what I've got for you:

1) **Acknowledge the banshee's banter**: Don't pretend the critical voice isn't there because it will only get louder. But then . . .

2) **Treat it with curiosity instead of criticism**: Don't beat yourself up for having critical thoughts, be curious about them. There is usually some retrograde self-preservation

function at work, so acknowledge that your inner voice probably has kind intentions but . . .

3) **Remember that voice is just another voice**: Hear it out, acknowledge it and then analyze it. Is what you are telling yourself objectively true? Is it based on unbiased data? Does it recognize the work you are doing to craft a future unshackled by the past? Sense check your inner voice's musings with your Ops Team too. They can help you regain that all-important perspective and fire you back up.

4) **Prove the voice wrong!** Many of us love to be contrarian (no I don't!) so when that voice in your head tells you what you're doing is stupid or will lead to disaster, or asks who you think you are to try to be somebody at your age, or questions why anyone from where you come from would be chosen as CEO, or blah, blah, blah . . . work your way through all of the steps above but then focus your efforts on proving it wrong.

5) **Do it for someone else**: And if nothing else works, keep going for someone else. When that voice starts taunting you about all the reasons you suck, how you will fail, how you will never do/become X, Y or Z, or how you are an impostor waiting to be unmasked who doesn't deserve to be in charge of a game of ping pong much less a global company, channel your Role Model Persona. Keep going so a colleague, a mentee, a partner, a brother, a friend or a child can see you doing your thing and know that it's

OK for them to do their own thing, too. Banshee banter
be damned.

Keeping Mission Creep at Bay

Unless you're willing to take Aristotle's approach to avoiding
criticism – 'be nothing, do nothing, and say nothing' – being
a leader, pursuing your Mission and living authentically as
yourself will require you to regularly grapple with outer and
inner criticism. Accept that hard truth, and now face another
one: no matter how great you are, to become your greatest,
you will have to make choices, often really difficult ones.

I used to struggle with this hard truth because in my
heart of hearts I am an unrepentant maximalist. I hate that
I can't have it all, be everywhere, do all the things and be
everything to everyone all at the same time. And it has
taken me a long, long time to accept the trade-offs inherent
in life but oh my, was it freeing when I did.

You might find this happens to you too. You pretend
like trade-offs don't exist. You love saying yes to everyone
and everything – you're that damned good! – and then find
you have nothing left for the things *you* care about. And no
matter how you try and no matter how much you 3D your
H-L-L-H quadrant or design the perfect Ops Plan, you
still get pulled into other stuff. Stuff that has nothing to do
with your primary Mission. Or, more insidiously, stuff that
has everything to do with lots of your secondary Missions.

When I was at business school, I knew that I wanted to start my own business. I was never short of ideas and had come up with many that vied for my attention. Divided Loyalties was an app that digitized loyalty cards into one interface and sent users alerts whenever they were near one of their loyalty card outlets, luring them in with special promotions. Your Life Story was a bespoke gifting service where customers could commission illustrated storybooks about their loved ones' lives. Flying Suds was a non-profit that salvaged toiletries confiscated at airport security and donated them to local shelters. I had notebooks bursting with start-up seedlings, and on any given day, I would flit from idea to idea, doing research about one before writing a business plan for another before entering a third into a competition. And day after day, my ideas stayed saddeningly static. And week after week, my ventures stayed needlessly nascent.

And then one day, my partner casually asked me, 'Which one are you going to choose?'

Which one? Which *one*?? Choose???

Fast forward ten years and guess how many of those businesses turned into something. Exactly none. Because guess how much of my undivided time and attention any of them got? Again, exactly none. But the two businesses that did go somewhere? Well, I'll tell you what was special about them, via a detour to Case Study Land.

I've worked with and advised a lot of can-do mofos in my life. And here are the differences I've noticed between the people who achieve, no matter how big or 'small' the achievement, and the people who keep talking about what they want to achieve:

While the talkers watch hours of mindless TV and pursue a seemingly easy life, the achievers put their plans into motion and keep going even when things are toughest. While the talkers hypnotically scroll through social media, the achievers consciously scroll through industry journals. While the talkers spend hours researching the hottest restaurants in town, the achievers invest hours researching the hottest mentors and advisors around.

And you know what else? While the talkers complain about how hard it is to catch a break and how the odds are stacked against them, the achievers create solutions and find alternative ways forward. While talkers curse the fact that they can't have it all and have it right now, achievers are clear-eyed about the trade-offs required by life and eventually get to have it all.

Now, some of you might be rolling your eyes and thinking these hypothetical achievers sound painfully boring but that is the point: success sprouts from the boring and the tedious. The most groundbreaking intelligence reports I ever contributed to required teams of us to sift through tens of thousands of discrete pieces of data for months on end before we struck history-altering gold. It took Edison one thousand failed attempts before he created a viable light bulb. It took Starbucks 16 years before it expanded outside of Seattle.

Success takes time. And it takes its *own* time. And that's why it eludes so many of us.

Because how many of us would continue to put in the effort even after hitting our first – much less first thousandth! – hurdle? How many of us would be so committed, so focused and so disciplined that success becomes an afterthought instead of an every-second obsession? How many of us would commit to the tedium of repetition instead of wishing for instant success?

I used to vacillate on a near-daily – sometimes hourly – basis between knowing that I needed to take consistent action on the right things (the tedium) and throwing my hands up in despair because the results weren't happening now (the success). But that's not how it works. Success at anything requires large stretches of boredom, sameness and F.O.C.U.S. ('following one course until successful' . . . not following all the courses!). And not everyone is willing to be bored or repeat the same thing, or focus.

That was my problem. I hated being bored. I came up with idea after idea because it was the fun and sexy part. Doing the doing was for the birds! But it wasn't until I started to commit and focus that I made any progress. And ten years and two *successful* businesses later, I can say for sure that the success only came because I took the sometimes-tedious track. I accepted the unsexy stuff for a while. And I ponied up the commitment and focus required.

If I can do it, so can you. You can commit to one Mission, to one vision, even when commitment is not instinctive. You can do what needs to be done even when you don't want to. You don't have to turn into an automaton but you do have to choose. You don't have to give up on everything else but you do have to make trade-offs. And one of those trade-offs will sometimes be trading excitement and variety for boredom and focus. That is life, my friends, and we are all grown-ups here.

But maybe, just maybe, if you can rinse off your mission creep-iest tendencies and learn to love focus and boredom even though it isn't sexy or exciting, success will take notice and invite you back to its place for the thrill of a lifetime.

Executive Order: For those of you who are still not on board with boredom, focus or making choices, let me be clear. You will not achieve anything important to you if you try to achieve everything. (This is particularly true for CEOs and leaders who have so many options to consider and decisions to make.) I get that you might be terrified of sameness and that variety is the spice of life and all that. But so is meaningful singularity. So here's a practical release valve that can harmonize those two competing realities.

Use the skills you learned in part one (3Ds, H-L-L-H, Ops Plan, etc.) to create boundaries for your variety and distraction needs. Give yourself an hour a day, or one day a week, or a weekend every two weeks, or one week every six months to flit and flirt and freewheel with other Missions/ideas/goals/visions/verticals. Allocate time and resources to be your variety-loving self, yes, but put a limit on the amount, so you don't sabotage your Mission-achieving self. Give yourself the gift of boundaries so you can sate your appetite for novelty while keeping yourself hungry for the main course of achievement. That is leading better.

Key Intel

- Comparisonitis can be Mission-killing and soul-destroying. To minimize its impact: compare apples to apples; learn from those you are comparing yourself to; remember what you *have* done that you are proud of; acknowledge that the path to success looks different for everyone; engage in something that makes you smile and externalise your feelings to gain perspective and objective input from others.

War Games

- You will be criticized – sometimes harshly and probably unfairly – when you pursue your Mission and live authentically as yourself. That is a universal truth so don't take it personally or use it as an excuse to stop continuing forwards.

- Your worst critic might be the one in your own head, so acknowledge that voice and treat it with curiosity – but remember it is just one opinion and you can prove it wrong.

- If you are tempted to give up on your Mission in the face of internal or external criticism, then keep going for someone else; you never know who else will be inspired by your example.

- Keeping mission creep at bay will be one of the hardest war games you'll play but trying to do everything and be everything will leave you with nothing. F.O.C.U.S. (following one course until successful) is the way to go.

- Give yourself time and space to engage with non-Mission things, too, of course, but create boundaries for how much time and space you give to those things so you don't dilute your chances of Mission success.

Chapter 7
Speaking Truth to Power

Case File: Stunned into Silence

When I was growing up, our lives were peppered with casual racism. People would shout 'go back to your own country', demand our Green Cards, ask when we learned to speak English, follow us around stores – all those nasty little reminders that signalled 'you don't belong here, and we are watching you'.

On our block, there were dozens of kids who my brothers and I routinely hung out with. We were laughingly U.N.-like in our diversity – Filipino-Americans, Indian-Americans, Jewish-Americans, mixed-race-Americans, Italian-Americans, Iraqi-Americans and lots of white kids who were not children of immigrants – but our crew was still tinted with racism. One of the white boys routinely stabbed me in the forehead shouting 'Hindu dot' (apparently, I later found out, he had a crush on me . . . how's that for effed-up playground politics!).

As I got older, the casualness continued: another white boy told me I was 'OK-looking for an Indian girl.' In high school, I went on a blind date where I was told the only other brown girl my date had ever found attractive was Princess Jasmine from *Aladdin*. A girl on my soccer team told me I was nothing like 'them' (all other Indian-Americans was the subtext) and said it was a compliment. What the fucking fuck?

But back then, I didn't say anything. I felt the tension of being wronged but not standing up for myself. I shrivelled up and rarely shoved back. From time to time I'd defend myself (or others), sure, but never as consistently as I wanted to. Because at the time, I had no concept that I could do anything but take what I was given. I thought I needed permission to stand up for myself (ladies, I wonder where we get that from? Oh wait, might millennia of being shut up and torn down and called shrill whenever we speak up have something to do with it?). And I thought it would be better not to make a fuss so people would like me, or at least benignly accept me.

I say again: what the fucking fuck?

Because I know better now, I *am* better now. I know that sometimes it is worth upsetting the accepted order of things. Sometimes it is worth using a battering ram instead of knocking on the door. Sometimes it is worth speaking up instead of shutting down.

But we have to *choose* our battles and our weapons. Not every fight is worth picking. Not everything we have to say needs to be said with the heat and intensity with which we feel it. And not everything we have to say is worth saying at all. Speaking truth to power isn't about grandstanding and soapboxing and haranguing. It is about choosing the right verbal tools for the Mission in front of us and unleashing our voices with the power and precision that can only come from choosing carefully and strategically. 'Choose your battles' is the mantra for this chapter.

Speaking truth to power was a Mission statement for us at the Agency but in most normal circumstances our instinct to use our voices is constantly undermined by society and custom. Children are ordered to do things without discussion. Adults interrupt each other constantly in 'conversations'. Women are routinely silenced by men. At school, we are given detention if we speak out of turn; at work, we are told there are certain bosses or clients we can't talk to because they are 'too important'. In pretty much every scenario we encounter from birth, we are reminded – explicitly or implicitly – of all the times we must be silent or risk negative repercussions. Amid all this shushing, is it any wonder that we often struggle to know when it is 'safe' to speak and when it is not? And is it any wonder that so many of us choose to stay silent instead of stepping onto the tightrope of talking?

But unquestioning silence does not a leader make. And in true leader fashion, we are going to get you finding and then unleashing your voice in a way that is true to you – respectful but not submissive and focused on the mission at hand. Using your voice powerfully and authentically will require artistry on your part, so I'll be sharing the fundamentals of the Art of Speaking, the Art of Asking, and the Art of Saying No. As you get more practised in each, you'll find that voice inside you blooming and pulsing and ready to roar.

Setting the Stage: Why Silence Feels Safe

Before we get going, let's look at why silence feels safe. For each of us, there is an internal and external matrix of signals conspiring to keep us shtum, and here are some of the signals I've observed that often go unnoticed (this is not an exhaustive list, by the way, so feel free to add to it based on your own experiences).

- **Obedience cultures:** All cultures around the world reward obedience over questioning in some way and to varying degrees. Witness what happens in most schools (knowledge is served up as truths to be swallowed instead of ideas to be engaged with); what happens in many families (kids being told 'because I said so' whenever they ask 'why?'); what happens in too many societies (citizens being subjected to rules they had no part in making). Wherever you live, whatever your national or family background, you could bore yourself to tears with examples of obedience being rewarded and questioning being punished.

- **The 'Regina George' effect:** Many of us will have experienced hierarchical pecking orders at school and found that to remain unpecked, we had to stay hidden and/or silent. The Mean Girls ruled the school and we internalized that it was safer not to call attention to ourselves or else we'd be emotionally tortured and socially cut down. So even as grown-ups, we accept hierarchies (social, political, ethnic, economic, professional, etc.) – no matter how unfair – to avoid being brutalized by them.

- **Family power dynamics:** What we experience in our families tells us from an early age who is or isn't allowed a voice, who is or isn't overruled and who is or isn't demeaned or diminished when they say what they have to say. Even in 'modern' families, more often than not it's the women who are silenced, subtly or overtly, by the men and younger siblings by the older ones (families have hierarchies too, says Captain Obvious). So as we grow up, however we identify and whoever's 'side' we're on, we pick up flashing bright signals about who is and isn't allowed to speak up. And because so much of adolescence is experienced in black and white, we too often internalize this in simplistic all-or-nothing terms.

- **The always-on-alert requirements of twenty-first century living:** We are constantly reminded of what a scary, terrible, terrorist- and now virus-infested world we live in and are asked to be vigilant all the time. From planes to buses to gatherings of any size, most routine and social activities come wrapped in all kinds of warning tape, putting our brains on alertness overdrive. Having to constantly scan our daily lives for threats siphons away essential life force and mental capacity that could otherwise be fuelling our vocal cords (or our Missions, or any number of things!). So is it any wonder that we have little energy or headspace left to speak up for ourselves when we've also got to channel energy into our work, our families, our health and lots of other things on top of being on high alert all day?

- **Our critical inner voice:** Yes, the one we went to battle with in the last chapter. She keeps resurfacing as the all-day DJ for Radio URSHT, playing classics like 'You Suck' and 'Who Do You Think You Are?' and the chart-topping 'Everyone's Going to Think You're Stupid', the follow-on hit-single to 'Everyone Will Laugh at You'. And instead of tuning into a different station (does anyone except a certain former US President have a station that incessantly tells them how amazing they are?), we turn up the volume. We tune in harder. And memorize all the words to all the hits and sing them to ourselves even when the DJ is taking a break.

So I ask you again, is it any wonder that so many of us find safety in silence?

> **Executive Order:** For all of you who are already in a position of power or leadership, you may be reinforcing the 'safety in silence' messages, so this Executive Order is a reckoning just for you (I warned you we'd be having some tough conversations!).
>
> Do you pay attention to the tone you are setting within your company or do you mimic leadership archetypes you've seen before? Are you intentional about the behaviours you reward or punish or are you replicating what has always happened? In meetings, do you welcome challenging questions or silence them? Do you surround yourself with sycophants or independent thinkers? Do you promote people based on capability or manipulability?
>
> Be honest with yourself. And then change what needs changing. You can reset the tone of deeply embedded obedience cultures. You can have tough conversations and learn from them. You can dismantle entrenched pecking orders. You can do all of this if you want to. Because you are the boss.
>
> So act like a boss instead of a bruised ego in the making. Give 'sexy' responsibilities to those most capable of executing them, regardless of seniority . . . or likeability. Ask for honest feedback and don't punish

those who share it. Solicit ideas that oppose your own. You don't have to implement what's suggested or proposed – you are still the boss after all – but you do have to recognize that good ideas don't only come from you. That being a good leader means listening even when the truth being spoken comes up against your power. And that obedience cultures are lazy but never easy.

So be a true leader and listen. Don't silence.

Finding Your Voice

Now that you know you're not alone – and that there are some powerful, if subtle, forces shunting you towards silence – let's get your Boss Badge back on and tell silence where to go. This is the part that requires finesse and artistry. You can't paint with a broom or build with a chainsaw, so let's make sure you choose the right tools that harness the right energy and channel it in the right way.

First the harnessing part. To gee yourself up to start speaking up when you'd normally back down, **tune in** to yourself. Remember all the times you clammed up. The comebacks you didn't come up with until it was too late. The big and small injustices that you let slide. What did you deny yourself? What did you deny others? What could have been the outcome if you had said your piece?

Take notice of those pain points and start imagining a different ending. Mentally replay a different outcome, one in which you stood up, spoke up or advocated for yourself or someone else. Keep it casual – or go over-the-top 'O Captain, my Captain' *Dead Poets* style if you want to – and just mentally explore what it feels like to use your voice for the things and people you care about.

Then **review the times when you *did* speak up** in the past. When you defended a colleague's idea. Or pushed back on a ridiculous client request. Or corrected a boss who kept mispronouncing your name (gosh, those moments are awkward!). Or stood up to your board. Whatever it was, no matter how big or small, there were times in your life when you were the hero or she-ro you needed to be. Funnel that power and experience into your Speaking Truth to Power Persona.

And **remember why** you want to use your voice. Do you want to get promoted or advance your career? Do you want to improve your organization or business? Do you want to stretch out of your comfort zone in your relationships? Do you want to advocate for a cause you care about? Do you want to champion others? Or drive change? Or share an idea that has gripped you? It doesn't have to be all the things! Using your voice isn't about verbally vomiting. It's about harnessing the power within you and speaking up about the things that matter to you when they matter most.

Unleashing Your Voice

From all this harnessing, you might start to feel an energy bubbling up or churning inside you in a specific location in your body (for me, the energy is always a big, fizzing orb in front of my sternum). Perfect! Because we're now going to help you unleash that energy with power and precision for the things you care about most, while accepting that you'll have to let some other stuff slide. Remember, 'Choose your battles' is the mantra for this chapter. (And ladies, please be particularly sensitive to the battles you choose whenever you are in a situation where you have to consider your physical safety.) Sometimes you have to tactically retreat from a battle to win the war and live to fight another day.

The Art of Speaking

Now, maybe you've found yourself in work situations where you had something to say but didn't pipe up for fear of looking stupid. Then, through some cosmic cruelty, a colleague said what you had been thinking all along and got applauded for the brilliant contribution they just made. What the eff?

Or maybe you've been to family gatherings where someone at the table makes an outrageous comment and you try to respond but immediately get talked over by your loud uncle. Instead of trying again, you give up and befriend the plate in front of you. (Families are notorious for perpetuating roles for its members, so if you were always the Quiet One good luck ever getting heard, right? No!)

It doesn't matter if it's in a professional or personal setting, we've all experienced wanting to or trying to say something but then stopping ourselves or letting ourselves be stopped. Think of the times when you've let that happen. Is that something you want to change? Is it a battle worth fighting? Are the work battles or family ones more important? Or do you have specific battles in each arena? You choose.

And after you choose, here's what you can do to start piping up:

- **Shut up to speak up**: I'm talking about Radio Station URSHT. Shut off that noise so you can start to speak up. It will get easier to do so when you . . .

- **Prepare and practise**: Rehearse what you want to say at that next board meeting, play out what you will do if someone interrupts you, say the words out loud, get into the right persona and prepare yourself with the information you need . . . and then practise, practise, practise. And while you are doing so, remember to **rehearse your delivery, not your anxiety.** You get what you focus on, so if you focus on your nerves, you'll get nervous; if you focus on your delivery, you'll deliver.

- **Deploy Tactical Ignorance**: We'll be getting into this in detail in Chapter 11, but for right now, tactically and tactfully ignore the context you're in. Don't get psyched out by how 'important' all the people in the room are, or by the presence of your boss, or the high-profile client. Ignore all that background noise and focus on delivering your message.

- **Start small and with low stakes**: If you're not feeling ready to jump straight into being a keynote speaker at your industry conference, start smaller and work your way up. Deliver the toast at a co-worker's going away party. Give a two-minute speech at your wife's fiftieth birthday party. Volunteer to lead the next PTA meeting. Keep an eye out for slightly less terrifying places that you can speak up and, as you get more comfortable and confident, work your way up to that industry conference stage.

- **Keep it light!** For goodness' sake, remember that your saying something isn't the be-all-and-end-all of anything. Maybe you speak up and it's well received (phew!) or maybe you say something and are met with a brick wall of silence (awkward!). Or maybe you say something and it gets acknowledged and everyone moves on (cool!) or maybe you say something and make a fool of yourself (oh well!). Whatever happens, keep it in perspective. And keep going.

- **And be you!** Use the medium that works for you and play around with different ones. If you are an introvert at meetings, write up the contributions you want to make and email them around before the meeting convenes. If you are terrified of a face-to-face conversation, take the bite out of it by role-playing with a friend. If you are a more intuitive person, don't over prepare (you'll know where your boundary is between just enough and too much). If you need to have a scary conversation over the phone, write out a script. Using your voice doesn't have to mean using your actual voice live and spontaneously. Sometimes a script, an email, a letter or a well-rehearsed speech can do the job.

But crucially, whatever you choose to say, whether at work or at home or with friends or with colleagues, you have to remember to adapt your message and how you deliver it to the situation at hand. In my CIA career, I briefed presidents, policy makers, aid workers, SpecOps units, decorated generals, ambassadors and everything in between. The overall message and analysis were always the same but the way I delivered them and what level of detail I shared was adapted to what *the audience* cared about and needed to know and how best *they* received the information (when President Obama once asked for a graphical representation of a written report – that's what he got!).

Speaking Truth to Power

The Art of Speaking is an art precisely because it requires you to be adaptive with how you deliver the message for the audience in front of you. So don't go to your boss to discuss a raise and wing it and don't go to your partner with holiday ideas laid out in PowerPoint slides, either (well, unless your partner's a management consultant; they seem to go ga-ga at the word 'deck'!). Choose your weapon for your target and remember that to reach them you have to speak *their* language.

The Art of Asking

Empathy and adaptability will be required in even higher doses when you start to ask for things that you deserve or want on a more consistent basis. Assuming you've picked your battles, the Art of Asking will still demand that you accept the inevitable fact that much, maybe most, of the time you will get a no. Life is a numbers game. So assume some knocks but also expect some kindness.

Sometimes you will tailor your message to perfection, prepare to exhaustion, rehearse your delivery to within an inch of your sanity and execute to the nine-millionth small detail . . . and still get refused. And sometimes you might do all of the above, maybe a little more, maybe a lot less, and get a yes before you finish your spiel. That is one of the maddening and amazing mysteries of life: no matter how much or how little you prepare there is always an element of chance involved (you catch someone on a good day, a bad day, an in-between day). But to give yourself the best chance of getting a 'yes', you still have to prepare: there are no shortcuts.

And by prepare, I mean make your request a no-brainer. Get inside the head of the person you are asking something of and frame your request in a way that serves *their* needs, so 'yes' is the only obvious answer. In sum: know your target.

If you need the managers reporting to you to step up their slipping performance, prepare for your conversations with them by investigating what might be causing their under-performance. Are there technical difficulties they're facing, personnel challenges, client issues or something else going on? Or consider having informal individual conversations – over coffee or lunch, say – to get some intel so you can frame your performance requirements to them in a way that speaks to what motivates them individually (professional reputation, contribution to the company, pride in their work, etc.) instead of defaulting to shouty-boss mode to scare them into compliance.

If you want a raise, ask your boss for it but go into the meeting with a detailed justification for why you deserve it in a way that speaks her language. List all of the tangible and intangible things you have done for the company that have made her look good (if she cares about that), that have made your group more money (if she cares about that), that have gotten your team industry awards (if she cares about that) and give concrete examples of how you have delivered again and again on the things she and the company value, on top of meeting all of the promotion criteria and performance standards.

If you want to convince your kid to eat veggies, prepare for that conversation by reminding yourself of what she cares about: running faster than daddy, being able to get to the top of the climbing wall, cycling without training wheels – and then remind her that veggies will help her build strong muscles that will power her running, climbing, cycling. (This works a treat with our older daughter!)

Or if you want to convince your partner to invest in some much-needed time away, get searching on all the amazing restaurants, or golf courses, or spas, or nature trails, or whatever he or she likes near your chosen destination and make your case based on what they will get out of the holiday. If your partner loves a deal, use any of the gazillions of deal sites and last-minute offer sites to snag something even they can't say no to.

The Art of Asking is about *the other person* at least as much as it is about you. And if you are genuinely interested in helping them get what they want, they are much more likely to be genuinely interested in helping you get what you want.

And even if you still get a 'no', remember that 'no' just means 'no, right now' and not 'no, forever and ever into infinity' (common sense alert: please don't twist these words for any twisted purposes; when it comes to sexual consent and personal boundaries no always and definitively means no). I have been told no the first time I asked for something but gotten a yes the fourth time. I have had a request rejected when I spoke to one person and then a yes when I spoke to a different person at the same company. Kids do this intuitively: they ask all the adults they can find until they find a pliant one. And we can throw some maturity into the mix and do the same in our careers and lives.

Go back with a different offer. Return with an enhanced pitch. Talk to someone different. Call at a different time of day. Try again a year later. Try again after the leadership team has changed. Try again when you have changed.

The negotiation – and all asks are negotiations – stops when you decide it stops. So regroup, reload and get back out there. Take an experimental approach. Collect data to see what landed well or what caused the other person to shut down. You might not get it right on the fifth or fiftieth try but each time you make an attempt, you will gather useful data that you can then use to readjust your strategy. This is informed persistence.

But please, please, please temper your persistence with sensitivity and good manners to make sure you don't become an askhole, either. Too many people don't follow basic courtesy when asking. They turn into badgering pains in the ass. Or suck you dry of advice/support/introductions/etc. and then sit on whatever you share. Or they hunt down help and never say thank you when they get it. What askholes!

Speaking Truth to Power

Don't let this be you. If you ask someone for a business introduction and you are lucky enough to get the introduction, don't sit on it. Pick up the phone or send that email to the person you have been introduced to. If you ask for advice and get it, don't simply throw it on the heap of things you know and never use. Apply it, filter it, reject it or tell the advice-giver what you did/didn't do with what they shared. If you ask a friend/a book/a community/the universe for some help and you get the help, don't take it for granted. Say thank you and reciprocate if and when you can.

And expect the same sensitivity and good manners from others who ask things of you. This will become even more essential as you become a leader, as you climb to the heights of your industry, and as you become more successful and more visible, because the sprinkling of asks you were once used to will suddenly become a blizzard. That is to be expected but don't be exploited. Get comfortable enforcing boundaries and saying 'no'. (More on that below.)

We have all been ask-ers and ask-ees. We have all taken others' time and given our own. We have all helped and been helped. It's an inevitable part of being a human. It's a great part of being a human. And it's a powerful part of being a human.

But with great power comes great responsibility – not to become (or let ourselves be abused by) askholes.

Executive Order: One thing I can predict with a high degree of certainty is that there are, or will be, times when you will stay fumingly quiet, not speak, not ask because you have imprisoned yourself in your principles. *'My idea is patently better; I shouldn't have to frame it in a certain way so the board accepts it.' 'I am clearly the best candidate for promotion, I shouldn't have to prove it to my boss.' 'I'm not the only one who can arrange playdates for our kids, my partner should just do it.' 'I shouldn't have to pay for food or drinks I didn't consume; we should pay for what we ate instead of splitting the bill.'* And on and on, you gorge on self-righteousness while cursing the world for requiring you to explain or convince or justify or ask for or state what is so obviously your due, what is so obviously obvious.

Well, dear ones, there is a reason engagement rings don't come wrapped in crumpled up newspaper nestled in cheap plastic bags: the packaging matters, the delivery mechanism matters. And if you want someone to say 'yes', if you want to improve your chances of getting the result you seek, you have to put in the effort to ask for it and make the proposition appealing to the other person. That is a fact of life, love and everything else that comes with interaction between humans. So keep your principles, sure, but don't let them keep you from achieving your goals.

The Art of Saying No

I have a confession to make: I am a people pleaser. I always have been. I was that kid in school who bounced in my chair with my hand thrust in the air to answer questions before the teacher asked them. I was that goody-two-shoes who bloomed under the gaze of adoring authority figures. I hoarded Es (for 'excellent') on my report card like other kids hoarded My Little Ponies. And that chronic pleaser syndrome has never completely gone away. So 'no' has always felt like a curse word to me. It feels icky. Bitchy. Mean. Selfish. Unbecoming of the teacher's pet. But as anyone who has less time than important things to do (and that is all of us, people – life is short!) will acknowledge, saying 'no' is one of the most essential arts to master.

The big and small things we say yes and no to have a measurable impact on our lives, our happiness, our success, our Missions, on everything. Being an adult – especially if we are adults who are also CEOs or leaders (or want to be one day) – requires using this super-powered word, and we can do so while honouring our most people-pleasing instincts by:

1) **Creating boundaries**: I used to devote entire days working on things I had yes'ed my way into that had nothing to do with my core Mission or anything important to me. I'd spend hours responding to emails (a.k.a.: other people's agendas), giving away free advice, looking over

other founders' spreadsheets or doing whatever was asked of me. I love to help and I hated saying no. But I very quickly realized that I was spending more time building other people's businesses than I was building my own! So I created boundaries: instead of responding to every random request for help, I created lots of free content (articles, YouTube videos, webinars, etc.) so I could help lots of people without having to respond to each individual. I allocated a set number of pro-bono hours to supporting a few budding entrepreneurs each year instead of taking all of them under my wing. I created boundaries around how much and how often I gave of myself, so I still had plenty left for me and my Mission. Creating boundaries allowed me to help others in a way that was sustainable and generous without leaving me vulnerable and exploited, and boundaries will do this for you too. So choose: how much, how often, how many, and then get used to . . .

2) **Enforcing the boundaries**: It's not enough to say you're no longer going to respond to every email from random strangers or will do no more than 200 hours of pro-bono work or will donate no more than 3 per cent of your salary to charities you care about each year. You have to enforce the boundaries. And this is the slippery part. It can be so tempting to say, *'One more hour won't really hurt'* or *'This guy's request is really endearing'* or *'It's only a fiver and it's a good cause'* or whatever excuse you will

try to make (I know because I have been there). But instead of looking for reasons to violate your boundaries, practise enforcing them. You can't help, save or serve everyone (I see you, fellow maximalists!), and trying to do so will dilute your impact. So once you define how much and how often you want to give, keep yourself in check! And get someone else to help you do so (your Ops Team can help you make sure you don't sabotage yourself). Because as a grown up you have to start . . .

3) **Accepting the trade-offs:** Whenever I talk about saying no and creating boundaries, people inevitably ask me, *'But what if you miss out on a potential opportunity?'* or *'What if the entrepreneur you turned away ends up building the next Amazon?'* to which I have developed the confidence to say with nonchalant conviction 'So what?' This is the only response you need to have. Life is full of trade-offs. Accept them and move on like the boss you are. And then get . . .

4) **Practising and putting together a script:** As with most things in life, saying 'no' gracefully, tactfully and authentically takes practice. Start small and work your way up. But start. And to keep yourself from backing away, have some scripts ready to go. If you know you will keep getting brain-picking requests from others in your industry until the day you die, draft an email template that you can send without agonizing over the next time such a request pops into your inbox (or, better yet, take

yourself out of the picture and have your assistant do it, or set up an email auto-responder). If you know potential clients will always ask you for freebies, put together a high-value freebie (one that is valuable but not business cannibalizing) and send it to them with a price list that shows what they will need to pay if they are serious about working with you. If you know you are going to say no to the PTA once you've hit your quota for helping at school events, write down what you're going to say when you inevitably get that call about Sports Day.

Saying no doesn't have to be painful. It might take time to get used to it, and it might require you to have some uncomfortable conversations, but you have to start doing it. Because for everything you say no to, you will release time/energy/money/resources/headspace/lifeforce to say yes to something else. To say yes to yourself. And to what is important to you.

Executive Order: I'm throwing in another executive order here because I know so many of you will resist saying 'no'. You'll want to say it and recognize the need to say it but still feel like you're being a selfish jerk if you do. So, let's get a few things straight:

1) Selflessness can get out of hand. We can be pushed to an extreme – internally or externally –

where everyone else comes first before we think of ourselves and everything else gets prioritized over our own goals and ambitions. That is a sucky way to treat ourselves.

2) There is nothing noble about self-sacrifice and there is nothing esteem-worthy about treating ourselves as afterthoughts. We have to take care of ourselves first, and – here's the hard part – we have to be OK with doing that.

It's not about being selfish or becoming a monster; it's about being self-full and becoming a role model. A role model who doesn't qualify or justify your deepest dreams or vision for yourself. A role model who doesn't make guilt into a fashion statement. And a role model who doesn't live with simmering resentment because you are always running on empty and running for something or someone else before even considering lacing up for yourself.

There's simple wisdom the aviation industry has been peddling for years: put on your own oxygen mask first before you help others put on theirs. And the same is true in all aspects of our lives. We can't inspire when we are suffocating. We can't do when we are drained. We can't pour from an empty cup. And we simply can't – shouldn't – make martyrdom and self-sacrifice our go-to move. (Others will put that on us anyway, huh, gals?)

So please, I order you, start filling your own basket (literally or metaphorically) before generously filling others'. Serve yourself the juiciest piece of turkey (literally or metaphorically) instead of settling for the shreds. Give yourself – and the world – the best of you by being self-full first, self-less second.

Key Intel

- There are powerful forces at play that keep us thinking that silence is safer than speaking up – accept that these forces exist and then move on.

- To find your voice, tune into the times you were silent, take notice of how painful it was for you, rehearse a different outcome (one in which you did pipe up!), think of the times you did use your voice for good, remember how that felt and remember your power, and then channel that Speaking Up Persona to use your voice as a weapon for good for the things that matter to you.

- Unleashing your voice does not mean verbally vomiting on people. It is about power and precision and choosing your battles.

- The Art of Speaking requires you to turn off Radio Station URSHT, prepare what you are going to say with the audience in mind, deploy tactical ignorance, practise with something small/low stakes and keep things in perspective while also keeping it you.

- The Art of Asking is about *the other person* at least as much as it is about you. Take an experimental approach, keep trying different things and learning from each attempt. Keep at it until you decide you are done but whatever you do, don't – I repeat don't! – become an askhole.
- Don't let your principles get in the way of your goals.
- The Art of Saying No might be one of the toughest arts to master but it is arguably the most important one. You can still be generous without being steamrolled. Create boundaries, enforce those boundaries, accept the trade-offs that come with being human and practise, practise, practise.
- And speaking of practice, practise being self-full, not self-less.

Chapter 8
When the Mission Goes Wrong

Case File: What Things Mean

At the end of my junior year of high school, I was at the top of my class. I was set to graduate as the valedictorian as long as I kept getting As and took on a rigorous course load in my senior year. So that's exactly what I did. I signed up for the most intense load I could take, enrolled in all the college-level courses my high school offered and got straight As in every single class.

And yet, on graduation day, I ended up giving the salutatorian's speech, the one reserved for second place (a.k.a. 'first last' as far as I'm concerned!). I wasn't the valedictorian. And I was devastated.

Now, mathematically speaking, there was no way anyone could have caught up with me, so I took the loss very personally. I interpreted it as a targeted injustice that had robbed me of a well-deserved accolade that meant so very much to me. And I carried an element of I-won't-get-what-

I-deserve-so-what's-the-point-in-trying-anyway defeatism deep within me for years after that. But the thing I realized with time, distance and maturity (thank goodness!), is that how we interpret what happens to us is entirely up to us. And things can mean everything or nothing or something in between depending on the story we choose to tell ourselves.

As a 17-year-old, I interpreted not being valedictorian as another example of the world having it in for me (this was also the reason I didn't have a mega-hot boyfriend and wasn't a supermodel. Being 17 was a never-ending exercise in suckitude!). But I could so easily have looked at it in a less charged way – as one data point of how the world works, but a data point that had nothing to do with me or my inherent worthiness as a human. Sure, I was just a kid, but so many adults think this way too.

My friends, in our careers, in our lives, in our Missions, things will inevitably go 'wrong' or turn out in ways that take no notice of our best efforts and that have nothing to do with us. Investors will act like jerks. Co-founders will suddenly get selfish. Product launches will fail. Suppliers will ignore us. Team members will abuse our trust. Partners will let us down. Kids will shut us out. And reality will take liberties with our timescales, targets and dreams. But how we internalize and interpret each of these things is entirely up to us. We can view them for what they often are (just a normal part of life) or as an indication of personal unworthiness and 'fated' failures. We can choose *'That guy was a jerk'* instead of *'I am not destined to be in a happy relationship.'* We can choose *'That was a disaster but I'll try again'* instead of *'It's not in my stars to have success and wealth.'* We can choose *'Them's the breaks'* instead of *'Fate is trying to destroy me.'*

I'm not suggesting we become delusional and absolve ourselves of all responsibility for what happens in our lives. Quite the opposite: I'm saying we can take ultimate responsibility for how we interpret what happens – regardless of who or what is at fault – and choose how we respond and what we internalize when 'bad' things come our way. Not everything means what we think it means. And sometimes shit just happens, whether we 'deserve' it or not.

We get to decide what things mean. We get to pick up – or leave on the floor – the damaging interpretations that will keep us and our lives feeling small. And we get to choose how we internalize – or not – everything that happens as we take ourselves to the heights we know we can achieve.

We will all inevitably face blowback at some point. But we can choose to blow back harder.

There are so many ways your Mission can go wrong and, at some point and to some degree, it will. The CIA coined the term 'blowback' to describe how, for every covert action, there was almost always an unintended or unwanted reaction. In more everyday settings, these messy and unwanted reactions are inevitable too. It's Newtonian physics; it's not personal. And none of it will matter anyway because in a few short pages you'll have undergone the mindset reset that will enable you to handle whatever messes and disasters seek you out. You will blow back harder.

As with so many things we've covered so far, a lot of the mess and disaster will come from within. You will sometimes be saboteur-in-chief. So in the pages ahead, I'll first help you get out of your own way and then help you reframe failure and tell F.E.A.R. where it can go whenever it tries to hold you down. The external threats you might face will be a cake walk after you get your head right because ain't no stopping the bullet train you are becoming, even when things go wrong.

Getting Out of Your Own Way

We clever humans have designed so many ways in which to get in our own way. We demand perfection from ourselves and give up when utopia eludes us. We overburden ourselves with how we 'should' be doing and how things 'should' be going, and then throw in the towel when reality proves otherwise. We sabotage ourselves and our Missions because we don't think we are good enough or worthy enough, or it won't last so what's the point? We think we are too old or are running out of time so don't bother to start. We erect barrier after barrier and put more energy into conjuring up reasons to give up than we do into going all in.

Many – maybe most, perhaps all – of us do some version of some of the above. So let's hack away at the massive mental blocks you've erected, slay the saboteurs you've littered on your own path, and get you back on track when *you* start making your Mission go wrong.

Internal Saboteur Number One: Paralyzed by Perfectionism

'If you want something done right, you have to do it yourself.'

Ahhh, the perfectionist's creed. I love these words because I can predict with almost 100 per cent-accuracy how many of you have them playing in a loop in your mind all day long. No one can close a sale as effectively as you can. No one can negotiate as well as you can. No one can draft an email as well as you can. No one can make lunch as well as you can. No one can order stationery as well as you can. No one can tidy up as well as you can. And no one can take out the garbage as well as you can, either. Isn't it amazing that you can do so many varied tasks better than any of the other eight-billion-plus humans who live on this planet or the few hundred thousand who live in your immediate vicinity or the tens of thousands who specialize in each one of these discrete tasks? Gosh, you really must be amazing! Right?

Hopefully you see what I'm doing here. Hopefully you've had a little chuckle while reading the preceding lines, not just because of how ridiculous they are when you see them written down but because you potentially recognize some of that silliness in your own way of thinking.

I get it. We love to be in control. We love to get things done. We love having things done our way (I basically wrote you a permission slip in Chapter 5 to demand as much!). And we are really, really good at some things, maybe even a lot of things. But perfect at all things? Is that even possible? The more I think about it, the more I see self-proclaimed perfectionism as something quite different: laziness and anxiety in disguise.

Let me explain. First of all, I think we can agree that doing anything 'perfectly' is basically impossible because 'perfect' is subjective. What I think is perfect, others might think sucks, and what they think is perfect, I might find seriously flawed. Perfect is a standard that we define and our definition will inevitably be different to someone else's.

Secondly, perfectionism is often used as an excuse for not doing something, for not pursuing or starting on our Missions: *That website will never be as perfect as I want it to be, so I may as well not build it'*, *'My business will never be as big as I want it to be, so I'm not going to start it'*, *'This mural will never capture everything I want to convey, so why bother painting it.'* Or perfectionism is used as an excuse to keep doing everything yourself because you can't be bothered to try delegating to someone else or letting go of something you've always done, or having a difficult conversation with a colleague or a partner about how they can contribute or improve. (I see you resisting all the hard stuff I've encouraged you to do!)

Perfectionism maintains the status quo – you either don't do something or you keep doing everything – and the status quo is, well, lazy. And perfectionism keeps you from addressing your often baseless anxieties. *'It has to be perfect or people will never buy it'*, *'No one will execute my vision as perfectly as I can'*, *'If I don't do it, it won't get done properly.'* Do you see how these perfectionist anxieties hold you back, keep you stuck and sabotage your Mission?

Do you think President Obama told the White House chef how to dice potatoes so he minimized waste? Do you think Sara Blakely orders the paper clips for Spanx HQ so they're not buying too many? Do you think Simone Biles spends hours online making sure she gets the quickest flight to the World Championships?

It's stupid for them to even consider those things!

So why do we? Why do we believe we can think bigger and lead better while still clutching onto every detail of leading and living? Why do we delude ourselves that we are the exception to every rule of success? (Delegate, leverage, focus on what you're good at . . . you know, everything I've been talking about for the past few dozen pages.) Are we really perfectionists or are we being lazy? Are we really perfectionists or are we just anxious?

Done is better than perfect. Trying is better than worrying. An imperfect business, a slightly meandering Mission, a half-baked but whole-hearted attempt is better than anything that stays locked in your head. Just get something out there; get going, get building, get executing and improve, iterate and – dare I say it – perfect it later.

You can't improve upon something that doesn't exist. You can't split-test a concept. You can't work out real-world kinks in a spreadsheet. It's only after you bring something to life that you can collect actual, actionable intelligence. Sure, it might feel sucky to put something out there that you feel isn't exactly right or to make an imperfect start on your Mission. But you know what's even suckier? Always wondering and never knowing what you could have been, where you could have climbed, what you could have achieved, how you could have thrived if you had hidden behind the perfectionist's creed a little less often.

Internal Saboteur Number Two: Shoulding All Over Yourself

Now that you're starting to wean yourself off so-called perfectionism, let's get into some hygiene. Because being a leader (of others and of yourself), pursuing things you care about and living your Mission will inevitably come with that uncomfortable feeling you get in your guts when you're shoulding all

189

over yourself. *'I should be growing my company faster', 'I should have fulfilled my Mission by now', 'I should stay friends with that person', 'I should read that book the marketing execs are talking about', 'I should . . .', 'I should . . .', 'I should . . .'*

Through all that shoulding, you will find yourself getting deflated, demoralized or even depressed at the litany of things you 'should' be doing but aren't. You will beat yourself up for lacking drive, energy, appetite and motivation, and suffer a slow bleed of distraction and frustration with all the shoulds ricocheting through your mind.

A big problem with shoulds is that a lot of the time, they don't come from you. More often than not, they're someone else's method, someone else's template, someone else's expectations and someone else's rules. They're externals that you've ingested and they are bloating your mind.

You feel you should offer a broader product range because that's what other businesses do, even though your customers just want three things. You think you should aim for seven-figure turnover because that's what 'real' entrepreneurs do, even though all you want is a profitable business that pays for your modest lifestyle. You tell yourself you should go on date nights each week because that's what other couples do, even though your marriage is full and fun without them. Should after should, expectation after expectation, you chip away at your essence and what is important to you. You get further away from what *your* Mission is about. You lose the reason you started down your own path. And you forget that being a leader means you can live by your own rules, instead of anyone else's.

I'm not encouraging you to go completely should-free (we're not about extreme diets here and sometimes advice/ best practice/ideas from others bear at least digesting and filtering) but I think we all know you've gotta dump some of the shoulds that are keeping you in the dumps. Often it's the small shoulds that have to go. One of the most liberating things I've ever done was to leave a social WhatsApp group even though I thought I should stay in it to be polite. The mental and emotional load I shed by doing that one small thing was massive; sometimes we don't realize how damaging and distracting the 'small' shoulds are until we've released ourselves from them. And sometimes it's the big shoulds that have to go, even if just for a limited amount of time. When I was bootstrapping my first business I kept telling myself I should be putting money away in savings. But in the early days of starting a business, every penny I saved had to be invested in growing my business or it would not have gone anywhere. So I released that should temporarily and consciously – and the associated stress of feeling like I was failing in my most basic of personal finance duties! – until my situation changed and I could re-impose that should.

Whatever combination of big and small shoulds you decide to do away with, remember that you are the boss of your own life and no true boss would ever suffer the indignity of senselessly shoulding all over themselves.

Internal Saboteur Number Three: You're Not Worthy

And speaking of indignities, we're now going to put the spotlight on some of the worthiness issues that you might be using to blow up your Missions before you embark on them.

So often when I'm advising founders or business leaders, little demons will creep into our conversation. They'll say things like, *'I'd do more to tighten things up but I just don't have a head for numbers.'* Or, *'I'm too timid for sales.'* Or, *'People like me don't get past a certain level.'* Or, *'I'm not supposed to be this rich.'* And that malevolent voice of doubt and despair murmurs to them every time they try to grow or do something that matters to them.

But these matter-of-fact 'truisms' that we repeat to ourselves and that keep us small or 'safe' are not always our own primal reflexes trying to protect us from disappointment (nor are they usually objectively true statements!). Often, the things that we tell ourselves we 'are' or 'aren't' are bits of mental baggage we've picked up from someone else. And it's time we give the baggage back so we can march unburdened on our Missions.

Sometimes it's the people who love us who load us down (this is why they don't always get a place on our Ops

Team!). The loving parents who told us to lower our expectations. The trusted teachers who insisted we set 'realistic' career goals. The dear friends who dismissed us as crazy for starting a business. And sometimes it's the assholes who throw on the load. The bullies who taunted us into submissiveness. The cruel exes who crushed our confidence. The aunts who told us we were stupid. And as we get older, the baggage builds and gets heavier, and then we throw our own on top, and before we know it, we are hunched down with our noses an inch from the ground when deep within we know we could be and are meant to be flying.

Whatever your I-can't-do-this-because mantras sound like, have you ever reflected on where those mantras came from? Are they from you? From someone else? If you're not sure, make a list. Quite literally sit down and write down all the damaging, minimizing and limiting things you've accepted about yourself as fact and then get scientific. What or who is the source of the belief? Is there any evidence to suggest otherwise? Have you disproven this 'truth' in the past? Or are you just cherry-picking the data to only confirm the negative?

You owe it to yourself to know why you think what you think. And you owe it to yourself to know why you shrink when you shrink. So if you suffer from I'm-not-worthy-ness and you know that it is tripping you up along your potentially glorious flight to Mission success, then get Homeland Security on your ass and X-ray the baggage you're carrying, scan it for destructive devices and destroy anything that you packed that someone else gave to you.

Internal Saboteur Number Four: Who You Have to Become

This saboteur is the matching carry-on to the you're-not-worthy baggage. So many of us have picked up cues, signals, comments and stereotypes throughout our lives about what people 'like us' don't or can't do, while also being flooded with equally stunting signals about success, wealth and fulfilment, and who we have to become to achieve those things. When we don't see ourselves in the archetypes we are given, we hold ourselves back.

For example, we're bombarded with messages that rich people are morally compromised and evil, so we subconsciously hold ourselves back from attaining material wealth because we don't want to be seen as – or become! – evil. We're beaten over the head with images of the side-parted, suit-wearing, shouty dickhead boss, so we hold ourselves back from pursuing leadership positions because we don't want to turn into a monster and have people hate us when we get the corner office. Or we're told people in certain industries all behave in a certain way so we don't apply for the job we really want in that industry because we're scared it will turn us into someone we're not.

But guess what? Money, leadership, job roles – none of that transforms you into something you're not; they can amplify who you already are, or keep you exactly the same. Your choice.

If you're a bit of an introvert and like to eat Domino's pizza, you can keep being an introvert and keep eating Domino's when you make your first gazillion. (It's just that as a gazillionaire, you could buy all the Domino's franchises in the world if you wanted to!) If you're kind and sociable, you can still be kind and sociable when you become CEO. (And now, your kindness and sociableness will radiate out to more people than before.) If you're fashionable and creative, you can still be fashionable and creative when you become an accountant. (And now you'll have the added glow of a person doing what they feel called to do!) Do you see? That is the power of Identity-Driven Leadership: everywhere you go, there you are. Not someone else. Not an impostor. Not a character you have to play. You. In all your complexity and uniqueness and wholeness.

So stop holding yourself back because you don't fit a false notion of who you have to become. Remember, you don't have to fit.

Internal Saboteur Number Five: Telling Yourself You're Too Late

I am someone who still struggles with the feeling that I'm playing catch up/running out of time, so this internal saboteur has particular resonance.

I remember a few years ago having a moment of panic. I had just put together a light snack – in this case pistachios, almond biscotti and *bhakri* (an Indian flatbread that is addictively delicious) – and as I tried to swallow my first mouthful, out of nowhere, a cascade of doubts and anxiety and nervous what-ifs started to choke me. *Holy shit*, I thought to myself, *I'm never going to get invited to Necker Island! I started my business too late!* (What the connection was between getting invited to Necker and *when* I started my business is beyond me, but then, irrationality doesn't make sense . . . duh!)

Why was I so consumed with Necker Island, you ask? Well, earlier that week, I had received not one but two emails from two different business founders telling me about their time at Necker. As I was trying to remember how to chew and swallow in the right order, my panic was escalating because I could not figure out how I would ever get an invite. And then Radio Station URSHT blared into action: *'Who do you think you are? (doo-wop doo-wop). You'll never go to Necker and Oprah won't ever want to talk to you (shoo wop dee dooo). It's too late for you (so just give up, deee dooo!) . . . '*

As the song was bringing me close to tears, I remembered a quote that always hauls me back from the brink: 'Never give up on a dream just because of the length of time it will take to accomplish it. The time will pass anyway.'

When the Mission Goes Wrong

The time will pass anyway . . .

And just like that, I was back in the room. DJ I'm-Gonna-Mess-With-Your-Head was off air and I remember thinking two things: 1) I have no desire to go to Necker Island so what was I getting so upset about? (Must be my comparisonitis flaring up again!) and 2) Stop crying and do something to move your business forward.

My friends, no matter how early or how 'late' you are in starting on your dreams, your desires, your Missions, your ambitions, the time will pass anyway, so for goodness' sake just start and keep going. Precisely because the time will pass anyway, wouldn't it be better to fill the time with trying, failing (because that shows you are trying) and taking mini, if terrifying, steps towards a dream or a goal? Sure, it might take a while for you to get where you want to go, or you might never get there. But you know what? The time is going to pass whether you sit on your ass and agonize about the things that won't happen because you're too old or too late, or whether you get out there and start making things happen. The. Time. Will. Pass. Anyway.

And you know what else? Even if you don't get 'there' (wherever 'there' is), at least you will have great stories to share and battle wounds to show off. And at least you will have tried. Life would be so boring (and saddled with regrets!) if we played it safe all the time, so why not just get out there and see what might be possible?

Everyone starts somewhere and sometimes those starts are 'late' in life; you wouldn't be the first. Boxing great Anthony Joshua started boxing at 18, which might as well be retirement age as far as the sport is concerned. Misty Copeland, the first Black principal dancer for the American Ballet Theatre, didn't lace up for the first time until she was 13 – the ballet equivalent of an old hag. Ariana Huffington founded the *Huffington Post* when she was 54 – 'late' by more standard measures, too. And how much worse off would the world be if any of the inspiring, hard-working, positive-contribution-making humans above had held themselves back by thinking 'I'm too old to do anything but retire and die.'

I'm not saying we all need to launch the next *Huffington Post* or become global role models in competitive sport and artistic expression. What I am saying is go out there and do your damned thing. Make stuff happen. Build your business. Send that first (or fiftieth) email to pitch your movie idea. Ask for what you want. Put yourself on stage. Whatever it is. Why not you? Why not me? Why not each one of us?

The time will pass anyway. And you're never too late, or too old, to start.

> ***Executive Order:*** The internal hurdles you'll throw at yourself are meaty and deep. So spend some time working through the ones that ring truest for you and

appreciate that in doing so, you might uncover other ways that you are holding yourself back. That is good. It might hurt and it might feel awkward, but until you know what you are up against, you can't chip away at it. So please, don't resist the internal work. It is the most important work you can do. You'll get better at sensing and stopping self-sabotaging behaviour and stunting beliefs before they trip you up but you have to remain vigilant to make sure you steadily shed your saboteur-in-chief title. That is one persona not worth stepping into anymore.

External Threats

Now that you're making progress with your mindset reset, let's start facing down the external saboteurs that will surely come your way. Because there will always be people who will try to make you fail, challenges that will get in your way and circumstances that will set you back. When that happens, the only thing you need to do is this: **Focus on what you can control.**

Simple, right? But it sure as hell ain't easy. Because who doesn't love a good wallow? Who doesn't love to blame someone or something else? Who doesn't like to bitch about the odds being stacked against them? It can be comforting to throw up your hands (if you're looking for an excuse to give up, you will always find one). But you don't have time to waste wallowing and blaming and bitching. You have things to do, mountains to climb, lives to live and Missions to accomplish.

So stop admiring the problem and focus on what you can control. Because the trade-offs are lurking: every minute you spend being angry is a minute you can't invest in being creative; every hour you spend being paralyzed by the problem is an hour you can't invest in finding a solution; every day you waste life force by wallowing in self-pity is a day you can't invest in making progress.

You will face challenges. You will face hurdles. And sometimes the challenges will come on top of the hurdles which will come on top of the setbacks which will sit on top of a pile of obstacles. I know this from experience. But guess what, you can choose what each of these mean and how you respond.

Sure, you can get angry at them but that won't make them move. And you can fume about them but that won't shift them either. Spend some time venting, fuming and getting the emotions out of your system (I am someone who needs to do that), but limit yourself to how long you'll be paralyzed by frustration and fury – and then move on. (I used to give myself a few days to wallow and vent, now I just take a few minutes.)

Working for a dickhead of a boss? Cool. Moan about him with your co-workers for a few post-work drinking sessions and then focus on what you can control: look into moving teams or jobs, stop letting him get to you, remind yourself that your job is funding your Mission, keep squirrelling away savings so you can leave one day, wait him out . . . but stop admiring the problem!

Got a business being buffeted by shitstorm after shitstorm? Great. Crawl under the covers for a few hours and cry (I've done that) and then wipe the snot away and focus on what you can control: write down all of the challenges, brainstorm potential solutions for each one, call your Ops Team buddies, talk to someone in the same industry, get advice from your accountant, do some research . . . but stop admiring the problem!

Having one of those days where there's too much to do and the curve balls keep on coming? (Been there, done that, got all the T-shirts!) Fine. Lock yourself in the bathroom for a while and then emerge ready to focus on what you can control: engage in a micro-dose of activity, ask your partner to take the kids out for a few hours, call an Ops Team friend, make a list of what needs to happen in order of priority and chip away at the list . . . but stop admiring the problem!

> **Top Secret Tip:** Micro-dosing activities will be one of the best sanity- and Mission-saving tools you can add to your arsenal. It is something I devised to get myself

through the first six months of first-time parenthood (when I was still working full time and never knew if my newborn's naps would last 20 minutes or two hours) and it is all about making progress in small increments of focused activity.

This is a hard thing to routinize because there is a lot to be said for long stretches of deep concentration. But 60- to 90-minute blocks of totally uninterrupted time don't always feature in the realities of our day-to-day lives. As a new parent, I found myself getting so frustrated that I couldn't carve out hours of productive time that I forgot how much I could get done by carving out minutes at a time. Big, important projects (or Missions) can feel like they can only be completed in big, important blocks of time. But that's not always possible.

But you know what is possible? Progress. While writing parts of this book, I've tweaked sentences in between making pancakes and waffles for Saturday breakfast. I've reorganized paragraphs for 20 minutes in the car while my husband drove us to our niece's rugby tournament. I've opened my computer to jot down an idea before shutting it down to go read my daughter to sleep. And yes, it has always taken a bit of time to pick up where I left off, get back into my writerly groove and make things coherent, but I made incremental progress in seemingly insignificant amounts of time that I would have otherwise thrown away. That's why micro-doses are so powerful: we make progress even under suboptimal conditions, even with suboptimal amounts of time.

But, as with so much else in life, the magic of micro-dosing isn't in the knowing, it's in the doing. Because doing something for a 'micro' five minutes a day translates into 1.27 days a year. Which means if we reclaim just 15 'throw away' minutes each day, we get back almost four days of time over the year (and four days is anything but 'micro'!). That is the magic of micro-dosing amplified by compounding.

So instead of getting frustrated with how much time you don't have, get something done in the time you do have. Not all projects lend themselves to being broken down, of course, and this isn't a map for how to work all the time or even most of the time. This is simply another tool to put in your arsenal so you can continue to move forward even when you only have a few minutes to spare.

So don't throw away the minutes. Make one phone call, write one paragraph, create one slide. Carve out large chunks of time when you can and use micro-doses of activity when you can't.

There are always, always, always going to be reasons to give up. And that is always, always, always going to be an option: you can give up.

But is that who you are? Is giving up an option for *you*?

Because if you're not going to give up (and you won't), then your only option is to focus on what you can control and keep going. Despite the suckiness. Despite the jerks who are trying to make you fail. Despite the odds being stacked any which way.

That's it. No magic. No secret sauce. Just persistence and perseverance. And controlling what you can control. Keep going.

> *Executive Order:* Now, look, neutralizing external threats will require effort and energy in micro-doses, macro-doses and everything in between, but do not senselessly, ceaselessly pound away at what's in your way, either. There are measurable and diminishing returns to doing anything for any sustained period without taking a break. Our minds simply cannot and will not function optimally without rest; our performance and ability to come up with solutions will suffer and accidents (or more problems) will result.
>
> So, while you are focusing on what you can control, also focus on controlling yourself. Don't overdo it. If you find yourself facing a brick wall, don't smash your head against it waiting for the wall to break. Take a break.

Go for a walk. Get some exercise. Consult with your Ops Team. Leave the problem for a while and come back to it later. You are immeasurably powerful and capable but you cannot force creativity. You cannot will solutions to appear. And nothing repels results as reliably as desperation.

And as for those assholes who try to trip you up because they want to see you fail? Being who they are is its own punishment. Your life and your Mission are about you, not them.

Reframing Failure

Remembering that your Mission is about you and no one else – not the saboteurs, not the assholes, not the competitors, not the critics, no one – is essential because at some point you will fail.

At the CIA, sometimes no matter how strong we were in the face of every sabotaging behaviour and problem that came at us, and no matter how focused and can-do and agile our response, shit hit the fan and rained down on our plans. But when those 'failures' came our way, we met them with a stronger, more resilient mindset and dealt with them, learned from them and reframed them.

Sometimes, no matter how strong you are internally or externally in the face of every sabotaging behaviour and problem that comes at you, how focused and can-do, and agile your response to threats, you will fail. Shit will hit the fan and rain down on your plans. But when those failures come your way, you can meet them with a stronger, more resilient mindset and deal with them, learn from them and reframe them, too.

Here's how:

Step one: assess the impact: When something goes wrong, what is the actual, practical impact? (Not the histrionic sky-is-falling assessment, the objective and practical one.) If your product launch failed, how big is the impact on your business's finances? What does that mean for your investors? What does that mean for your customers? Maybe nothing, maybe something. Define the impact, make it concrete and quantify as much as you can.

Step two: decide what it means: Again, leaving theatrics aside, what does the 'failure' mean? If you failed one of your CFA exams, does it mean you're a failure as a human? Or does it just mean you have to take the exam again?

Step three: choose what to do about it: What steps can and will you take to mitigate the impact of the 'failure'? For the product launch, can you cancel remaining production? For the exam, can you take it again?

Step four: learn from it: As Churchill famously said: 'Never let a good crisis go to waste.' Fail but learn. What could you have done differently? What will you do differently next time (test new products on focus groups before launching, invest more time studying without multitasking, etc.)?

That is it: Fail. Fall. Get up. Learn. And try to do better next time.

As anyone who has gone to business school can tell you, there is always a failure-ridden story behind every glorified success. In business school case studies, the 'A Case' delivers glowing narratives about how a business grew seamlessly, hopping from strength to strength until one magical run-in with the perfect investor skyrocketed the start-up from basement office to Silicon Valley darling and the founder made trillions along the way.

The 'B Case' lifts the curtain on the made-for-pop-culture facade and describes in detail how each 'strength' was just a string of right place, right time good luck and that perfect investor was the 900th investor the founder approached. The 'overnight' success took 12 years and two divorces to come to fruition and the founder worked herself into the hospital because she forgot to take care of herself along the way.

Same story, both true, different focal points.

So what I am saying is: choose your framing. You can focus on the A Case interpretation, the B Case, the C Case, or anything else. Failure can just be a thing or it can be The Thing. Success can just be a thing or it can be The

Thing. (Or you can take the Rudyard Kipling approach and view both triumph and disaster as impostors that have nothing to do with your inherent worthiness as a person.)

Decouple your identity from the results. Sure, you can work towards successes and achieve them or suffer from failures and do nothing to 'deserve' them, but they will happen just the same. As my dad once told me: 'Sometimes, no matter what you do, you won't get anything right and other times, no matter what you do, everything you touch will turn to gold.' No matter what you do.

So choose what things mean and reframe the outcome, without always defaulting to the negative. Do what you can do. And just keep going.

Taming F.E.A.R.

As you work to reframe failure, you will confront its favoured friend: fear. Fear will try to keep you small, trip you up and make you lose sleep. Fear will make you doubt yourself, stop yourself, limit yourself and give up on yourself and your Mission.

When I was still a new(ish) parent, I flew from London to New York with our then-toddler. It wasn't fun but it was finally over after a few tears (mostly mine), lots of internal screams (again, mostly mine), copious amounts of silent cursing (very definitely mine) and seven hours of pacing up and down the aisles. I had been terrified in the run-up to our trip because I had never travelled with our daughter alone and seven hours in a confined space with bad food is a big ask of most people, much less an active tot. But in the end, it wasn't that bad and we got through it together without any meltdowns, and at least one of us was still smiling happily when we landed.

One of the lessons I learned (again) on that flight – I seem to learn this lesson a lot, by the way – is that the fear and anxiety I'd felt in anticipation was a poor prediction of the reality. That F.E.A.R. is often nothing more than False Expectations Appearing Real. (And that it was stupid to even consider limiting my transcontinental travel just because I had a toddler.) This happens so much in our lives and in pursuit of our Missions. We wind ourselves up into Gordian knots worrying about things that haven't happened and waste precious head space and brainpower and life force anticipating vague disasters instead of rehearsing the disasters (as we learned to do a few chapters ago) or recognizing the false-ness of our real-appearing expectations.

I would have to rely on some high-order math if I tried to calculate the number of times I have anxiously expected disaster or suboptimal outcomes before an event, a speech or just a phone call. I know how hard it is to keep a leash on rabid fear. But with time and experience, and each new thing that goes better than I'd fearfully anticipated, I have started planning for success just a little bit more. Anticipating happier endings. Letting my mind roam through *best-case* scenarios a little more often. And going ahead and making stuff happen despite my fears.

Most of us can survive even our worst imaginings, so why waste the time imagining them? Why waste an opportunity to prove something to ourselves when fear is often no more than a false expectation appearing real? I know it's not easy, but it is doable.

If you can't always do it for yourself, push past your fears for someone else, so that those who are watching (and someone is always watching) can see that fears are not something to give in to. Life is fraught with daily 'terrors' (public speaking, analyzing financial statements, asking for sales, launching a product, forging new relationships, learning something new) but we can choose to be brave for our audience, our investors, our clients, our customers, our families, our employees, our Missions when we can't be brave for ourselves. It doesn't matter who or what we are being brave for, just that we are. We still get the benefits even though we aren't the intended beneficiary. We still get to prove to ourselves that we are capable of more than we realize. And we still get to feel the power of who we are, who we are becoming, when we hold our fear without letting it hold us back.

Key Intel

- All Missions are riddled with challenges, that's just life, but the biggest challenges will be the ones you set up for yourself.
- Work on overcoming your perfectionism (laziness and anxiety in disguise!). Stop shoulding all over yourself or telling yourself you're not worthy or that you have to become someone you're not. And remember, you are not 'too late' or 'too old'.
- When you meet external challenges and hurdles, don't admire the problem. Focus on what you can control and do something.
- Choose what 'failure' (and 'success') means.
- Remember that F.E.A.R. is often False Expectations Appearing Real. If you can't be brave for yourself, then be brave for someone else. There is always someone looking to you as a role model, whether you realize it or not.

Part Two After-Action Review

Well, hello there. In just a few short chapters, you've stepped into your Identity-Driven Leadership style and started to go to war with all manner of inner and outer traitors. This is tough stuff and you've toughed it out.

You're having difficult conversations, using your voice and dealing with stress and worry like a boss. And you are committed to bossing it forever more because you know that this is just the beginning and the work never stops (especially the internal work). But you also know that you get to choose when to stop and when to keep going. You get to decide what problems mean. And you get to reframe everything that happens, or doesn't happen, because your self-worth has nothing to do with those twin impostors: success and failure.

Bossing. It.

Now that you're consistently Thinking Bigger and Leading Better, let's bring your bigger, better self out into the world in a more visible and powerful way. In the section ahead, I'll be guiding you to be bolder in everything you do, as I trained myself to do when I left the Agency and built my business career from scratch. I'll be showing you how to leverage the foundations we've laid together to step out of the shadows and into your light, and push yourself further and higher than you ever thought possible by being seen and heard on a bigger scale. Watch out world, here you come.

Part Three
Being Bolder

Chapter 9
Stepping Out from the Shadows

Case File: Don't Wait to Be Discovered

When I was a teen, I heard somewhere that Kate Moss had been discovered by a modelling agent at an airport. So, for years after that, every time I flew, I would get breathless with desperation for some talent scout to pluck me from the travelling masses and plaster my face on billboards and magazines. Even after I stopped dreaming of being a model, that idea that I had to 'be discovered' stuck with me. I wasted a good few years of my life, even as an adult, waiting to be chosen, wishing for recognition, waiting for nominations and wishing for accolades. And I wasted even more of my life feeling deflated when they never came.

What an idiot.

Because what I realized with time and experience is that the world doesn't work that way. We are led to believe that if we are good at something, if we have something to offer or we create something worth sharing that others will magically find out about and turn their attention to us. 'If you build it, they will come,' and all that.

But that is utter nonsense.

A lot of the time, the people on things like Forbes' lists get on there because they apply to be on them. Often, the companies that win awards are the ones that put themselves forward for the awards. And the people who get noticed are the ones who call attention to themselves. These companies and individuals are not 'discovered'. They do the work and give themselves a chance, instead of relying on chance.

If I had really wanted to be a supermodel all those decades ago, I should have got a headshot, gone to auditions, thrown my hat in the ring and done the work – and kept doing it and kept auditioning – instead of being passive-depressive about it. The same is true for all of us. Because as wonderful as we may be, and as much as we may do and have to offer, no one else is keeping track. No one is tallying all the amazing things we accomplish. No one is funnelling to us all the things we may deserve. And they (almost) never will.

Over the past few years alone, I have donated over 800 hours of my time to my various alma maters through pro bono mentoring and workshops. Is anyone chasing after me to give me a medal? Is anyone nominating me for an award? No and no. But if there is ever an opportunity to nominate myself, will I do so? Yes. Of course. Does that make me a self-promoting jackass? No. Because I did the work.

Stepping Out from the Shadows

I volunteered the hours. I didn't do it so I could get recognition but if the opportunity to be recognized arises, then I'm going to recognize myself for how much I contributed and put myself forward.

That is what we all need to do. If you did the work, apply for the award. If you meet the requirements, put yourself forward. If you lived the experience, pitch for the story. If you have the product, ask people to buy it.

There is nothing holy about obscurity. There is nothing holy about anonymity. And there is nothing *un*holy about not staying obscure or anonymous. So put yourself forward. Put yourself out there. Put yourself in the race. It doesn't mean you will be recognized. But trying sure as hell beats waiting for someone else to discover what is wonderful about you, your business or your story when you already know.

At the CIA, most of our Mission successes had to remain hidden. There were clear and compelling reasons to make sure that the work we did remained secret. But even though we couldn't plaster our achievements on billboards, we knew what we did and we celebrated in the shadows. But you, my dear readers, are not engaged in top secret missions. You have no reason to hide (aside from the internal blocks and external baggage that you've now started to process and dump in the previous chapters). You are not protecting national security by staying small. So it's time to step into the light. Because you, your story, your successes and your Mission milestones are worthy of a spotlight. And what you have to offer the world needs to be known.

As with everything we've done together, we are going to be you-focused when getting you out there to shine. Not forcing you to be someone you're not but expanding your sense of how much being seen and heard feels right, and doing it in your own way. Because, let's face it, when you become a boss, a CEO or an expert in your field, or are simply really good at your job, you will get attention, and bossing your life means making sure what people see is authentically **you**.

A lot of people carry a lot of baggage – as we now know, usually someone else's – around being more visible, taking pride in their story and letting themselves shine. They think profile-building somehow cheapens their work and that telling other people what they do or how good they are at it tarnishes their integrity. But, as I've said before about lots of things we blindly accept, that is total horseshit. Becoming more visible doesn't mean you have to be full of yourself or get in other people's faces. You choose how much you want to shine and how brightly, and whether other people are blinded or dazzled is up to them. You just focus on doing you.

Together, we'll get you taking pride in your story, letting yourself shine, building your profile and fine-tuning your personal presence. As you start to own your value and share it with others, you'll find yourself reaching people who resonate with your message and helping people you never realized you could reach or help. And you'll find yourself being recognized for what you already do or getting promoted, or headhunted, or praised, or written about . . . or just feeling the glow that comes from no longer hiding your light under a bushel. All great things!

So take that first tentative step out of the shadows and stop waiting to be discovered.

Executive Order: Visibility can feel particularly fraught for leaders and CEOs who consider themselves private, introverted or who shrink in the limelight. But the thing is, you don't have to be an extroverted gregarious type to lead or succeed. The archetypal charismatic, suave, fast-talking, hard-charging image of a leader we've been force-fed by Hollywood and popular culture has nothing to do with reality. The worlds of business, politics, academia, the arts – every field of human endeavour – are full of examples of great leaders and paradigm-shakers who are internal, quiet, deliberative and thoughtful.

There are lots of different ways to be a leader – duh! – so if being visible isn't your thing, fine. This chapter is about being seen and heard *your* way. So, if big company-wide town halls aren't your style, no sweat. But can you have one-on-one chats and walk the halls from time to time to get a pulse on what's happening within your company? If fist thumping motivational speeches aren't your forte, cool. But can you send a carefully crafted email or video of you sharing your thoughts instead? If endless meetings are a distraction from important thinking time, I hear you. But can you get your assistant to protect time away from meetings for you, or have your chief of staff run interference while you go into your metaphoric cave? You have options. You are the boss.

But – harsh reality alert – being a leader also means that you'll have to work in your discomfort zone from time to time and that includes being more 'out there' than you may want to be. You'll just have to suck it up and do it. But the tips I'll be sharing in this chapter will make sure you can do it your way. On your terms. And as your own authentic self.

As we walk through the exercises, think of how you can apply them to some of the being-seen-and-heard tasks you shrink from. How can you make it easier on yourself? How can you adapt the situation to fit who you are and how you operate?

You can't always avoid the public eye but being thoughtful about how you are seen and heard will enable you to bear it. Because you'll have to. And because you can. You've got this. We've got this together.

Becoming More Visible

Every single founder and leader and individual – regardless of age, industry, gender, background or confidence-level – who I have helped become more authentically visible has resisted it like I was asking them to walk naked through the streets shaking pompoms and shouting 'Look at me!' from a bullhorn. (I can sorta see why: being visible can certainly *feel* exposing and exhibitionist, but not the way we do it; we've got more grace and class than that!)

If your Mission or ambitions include some element of wanting to change the world for the better, help other people, improve your community or simply improve your own life, being more authentically visible will help you do all that . . . and perhaps even more.

Why blow your cover?

Think about how being more visible, building your reputation and being known for what you do **can help you reach your goals and/or serve your Mission**. Circle all of the reasons that resonate for you below and feel free to add your own.

By becoming more visible you can:

- become a powerful advocate for causes you care about
- drive change
- progress your career

- get recruited by firms you want to work at
- attract customers and clients
- share ideas
- get recognition for your expertise
- raise awareness about important issues
- something else (be specific!)

There are no right or wrong answers, so invest some time thinking about how you could help yourself and/or others by being seen and heard more widely.

Part of what pushed me into my discomfort zone of putting myself out there was that I wanted to help as many people as possible. Remember all those founders and leaders who kept pinging me for advice or help? Well, I realized I could reach all of them – and many more founders and leaders and individuals besides – if I started putting my insights online. I hated the idea of social media, but I hated the idea of not helping people more. So, armed with nothing more complicated than my laptop, a five-year-old smartphone and an amazing VA, I started creating and posting videos, blogs and think pieces online. And in doing so, I was able to talk to far more people than I would have ever been able to otherwise.

And the other reason I forced myself to be more public (I am an extrovert but also intensely private) was because I wanted to be an example to encourage other women to get more comfortable being more public, too. Visibility, for me, is as much about challenging the default invisibility that is far too often foisted on women as it is about positive impact. It's personal and political.

Women's contributions are still left out of the history books (women like Katherine Johnson, who was a 'Hidden Figure' until the book and movie with that name came out), our successes are still maliciously subtitled ('she only got here because of a quota', 'they loosened the criteria for her', 'she slept her way to the top') and, maybe worst of all, when we do achieve something, our gender is always there to qualify it: we are a 'female founder', a 'woman CEO', a 'mompreneur'. The message always seems to be that, syntactically and practically, being a woman comes first, our achievements sit second.

Part of why I work so hard to help others become more authentically visible is because I want to normalize success and visibility for all previously marginalized achievers and doers. And that is why we all need to shine as brightly as we can. Why we need to celebrate our successes. Why we need to tell others when we've won an award. Why we need to share the magazine articles or podcast interviews we are in. And why we need to put ourselves out there again and again. This isn't to say we become obnoxious self-promoters (though maybe we allow ourselves to be just a little bit 'self-promote-y' ...) or that we blow our trumpets without substance to back it up. It *is* to say that we get more comfortable talking about the amazing things we are doing because we deserve to be included in humanity's records.

When we shine without apology or qualification and with honesty and honour, we give others – women and all of the other quieter or ignored achievers – permission to do the same. The world desperately needs more diverse (there, I've said the d-word) role models and one of those role models is you.

Taking pride in your story

So how do you do it? How do you share and shine and show up? Well, first you have to know that you have something worth sharing. And if no one has ever told you that, I'm saying it to you now: **you have something worth sharing**.

What that 'something' is precisely might be obvious or it might be hidden, so mine yourself. Dig deep, sift through your life, pan the insights and discoveries you made in Part One and bring your treasures to the surface. Sit down and reflect on everything you know and everything you've experienced that might help you or someone else:

What are you known for?

What do people always ask your advice about?

What qualities and strengths come up during professional performance reviews?

What positive feedback have you received from friends, partners, co-workers, bosses?

Stepping Out from the Shadows

What do you know you are good at?

What expertise do you have?

What do people always compliment you on?

Look at both 'hard' and 'soft' skills and start to make a list. Expand upon your Backstory question four answers (see page 20 for a reminder) and identify at least ten tangible skills (accounting, writing advertising copy, public speaking, etc.) and ten intangible skills (negotiating, connecting people, thinking strategically, etc.). If you struggle to get to ten, ask people who know you and who you trust to give you some candid feedback on your strengths and skills. I did exactly that when I was transitioning out of business school and into my entrepreneurial adventures: I asked a select group of people who knew me really well at work and socially to fill out an anonymous survey, and the insights I got from them refined my approach to how I ran my future businesses, confirmed what I thought were my strengths . . . and contradicted what I thought were some of my strengths too! Mining yourself and asking for candid feedback will inevitably bring up coal as well as gold – that is the point. Accept the coal and polish the gold.

Letting Yourself Shine

Now that you have started to see just how much gold lies within you, start letting that gold shine. The things that come easily to you, the things that you are great at, the things other people see as your superpowers, they are all valuable because there will be other people who want to be good at those things, too. So start sharing those things. You are not beholden to the National Security Act, so stop acting like everything in that overflowing brain of yours has to be kept under a tight lid!

You have a literal wealth of knowledge that could benefit other people's lives (or your own life) by sharing it, so stop being such a hoarder. Decide which of your skills or attributes you want to share, who you want to share them with, and why your message matters to them, and then start sharing your message in the places your people hang out.

If you are a business consultant for early-stage founders, you can start sharing some best practices on how to raise seed funding on Instagram where you know your niche of founders are scrolling on their lunch breaks.

If you are a tax consultant who specializes in R&D credits for small and medium size businesses, you can start sharing some top tips on LinkedIn, where you know your target customers are searching for professional service providers.

If you are an amateur stained-glass artist, you can start sharing ideas for how aspiring artists can make their own stained glass by posting videos on YouTube, where most people go for visually supported 'how-to' advice.

The possibilities are endless. And so are the media at your disposal. You just have to start seeing, listing, and acknowledging all the things you are really good at and then start sharing it in a way that feels right to you and helps you get closer to one of your Mission or life goals.

This will be an experiment so don't presume anything. I used to run away from cameras but found that I love doing YouTube videos, so I stopped running away. I used to cringe at the sound of my own voice (it really is bizarre how different we sound in our own heads compared to how we sound when recorded) but found that I love hosting podcasts and being interviewed, so I got over the cringiness.

Your end goals, what you want to achieve, who you want to help are more important than how you think you look or sound, or whatever hang-up you have, so give yourself a chance. Try different things. Try writing or blogging or vlogging or podcasting or photographing or video-making or whatever. But just try. You will surprise yourself.

And once you put your stuff out there, forget about it! Don't obsess over it. Don't go back and make tweaks. Don't overanalyze every eye twitch or comma or thing you think you screwed up. Put something valuable out there and leave it alone.

Seven Steps for Sharing Your Story

As you edge your toe into the spotlight (I know it feels awkward after all that spy-training you've done, but you've got this), you will need to experiment with what feels right to you and you can use these seven steps to get you started:

1. **Don't preach**: Even if what you are saying is authoritative, you don't have to lecture. You can avoid this trap if you . . .

2. **Tell a story**: It can be about how you got really good at something, how you arrived at a certain personal or professional milestone, what things you learned on the way towards a certain achievement, the thoughts that go through your mind while you are creating, the frustrations you encounter in your day-to-day life and how you overcome them, the funny moments you have as a parent, the ah-ha moments you've had as a specialist consultant . . . Whatever you decide to share, the best shares often **inform, entertain, inspire** or combine the three in different ways.

3. **Use your voice**: You don't have to try to be or sound like someone else. This is about you, and how you want to show up. So just because everyone else who shares marketing tips on Pinterest does so a certain way, doesn't mean you have to. Play around with your voice, your style, your tone, and see what you are naturally drawn to as you.

4. **Start small**: Being more visible can feel overwhelming if you're not used to it (and even after you are), so start

small. Set yourself a goal of doing one post a week, or one video a fortnight, or one podcast episode a month, or whatever frequency is just outside your comfort zone but not so far that it keeps you from doing it at all.

5. **Keep it light**: The comforting paradox about being more visible is that everyone is watching but no one is really watching. Some people may pay attention and take notice; others will anxiously await your next foray into the light but a lot of people won't even realize you're there. Take comfort in that and just keep putting your valuable stuff out there.

6. **Stop shoulding**: Other people in your industry or with your talents might post every day on dozens of platforms and have slick graphics and perfect copy and hyper-produced podcasts and professionally edited videos and shiny business cards, but that doesn't mean you have to. You get to choose and you make the rules for how, where and how often you show up. As long as you are consistently sharing something of value to your audience, what other people 'like you' are doing doesn't matter. Just do the best with what you've got – time, resources, etc. – and know that that is enough.

7. **Be consistent**: Yes, you get to make the rules for yourself but that doesn't mean you get to make no rules for yourself! If you want to be visible you have to show up consistently, so decide a schedule, a medium and a format

that works for you and then keep showing up that way and that often. You can make tweaks later but you have to get started with some structure.

Executive Order: Once you decide to put yourself out there in support of your goals or ambitions or Mission, tell everyone what you are doing (you're writing a blog about insect genealogy, are leaving your law firm to master gelato making, etc). Tell your favourite barista, people you chat with on the train, friends who you assume know everything about you (they don't and sometimes they don't pay attention), colleagues (as long as there are no conflicts of interest with your day job), parents at the playground, fellow dog walkers, everyone.

Do it gracefully and appropriately but tell people what you are doing even if you haven't started doing it yet. You'll create Mission magic in two ways:

1) If you haven't started yet and/or are procrastinating, telling people will create motivating pressure to get off your ass and do something because now other people think you are doing it (more on using 'targeted leaks' for accountability in Chapter 12).
2) Every encounter is a potential lead and a potential source of insight so don't rob yourself of serendipity's superpower. Businesses have been built on the

---

backs of passing conversations between strangers. Careers have been skyrocketed after chance encounters with unassuming connectors. Plays have been written on the inspiration received from randoms.

Tell everyone what you are doing and let the magic happen.

Profile-building

Once you've decided to put yourself out there and tell everyone about your Mission or message, you will also need to run a parallel op that builds your personal and professional profile.

Your profile is many things. It includes what people get when they look you up online or follow you on social media; how you show up when you are at work, speak at an event or attend a conference; and what people say about you as a person and professional. Most of these things are within your control – baseless gossip and haterism doesn't count – so focus on these.

First, audit what's already part of your profile and then tighten up anything that needs tightening. Once you do that, then the real fun can start as we get you seen and heard more widely.

Social Media: Audit

I'm sorry to tell you this but people will google you. Whether they are a recruiter, an event organizer, a potential client or your kid's friend's parents, we humans like to suss each other out. And that's why it's important to know what your social media profiles are saying about you. You control these profiles, so whether they say nothing or something is totally up to you. But once you decide you want to be more visible, then you need to make sure that the platforms where your target audience lives are where you are most active and that your profiles there are the fullest, you-est they can be.

Let's say you are looking to gain followers on Pinterest for your marketing mastery secrets. What does your Pinterest profile look like? Is there a photo of you? Or of your client campaigns? What useful content have you shared? Have you engaged regularly with your audience of master-marketers-in-the-making? Do you have a call to action of some sort ('follow me', 'read my pdf guide', etc.) and is it clear to people what you are good at?

Or let's say you are desperate to change jobs and know head-hunters for your industry regularly scour LinkedIn. What does your LinkedIn profile look like? Do you have a professional profile photo (not a selfie!)? Are you regularly posting about trends you've noticed in your industry? Are you engaging with relevant colleagues on the platform?

Does your profile mention any of your credentials, awards or certifications? Is it clear to those recruiters what you are good at and how you are different?

Wherever you are trying to raise your profile, make sure you ask yourself a few questions:

- What are you saying?
- What does your profile say about you?
- How could you beef up your profile to attract your target audience?
- Do you engage regularly?
- Is your message coherent?
- Is your message consistent?
- Is your message appropriate for the platform?
- Do you have a call to action?
- Are you shining or hiding your light?

Social Media: Tightening

Once you know what your profiles currently look like (or don't), take the next step and improve them (or create them from scratch). Get advice from people you trust. Ask your Ops Team to weigh in if they are qualified to. But don't pretend it doesn't matter.

At the CIA, we had an unofficial litmus test called *The New York Times* test: if you were ever torn between various courses of action, take the one that would cause least embarrassment or trouble if it showed up on the front pages of *The New York Times*.

For your purposes, use the Google test. If someone were to google you, would you be embarrassed or proud of what they found? Use that as a guide to tweak, refine and improve your various social media and other public profiles.

Personal Presence: Audit

As we talked about in Part One, your personal presence matters, too. A lot. People who meet you in person will form snap judgements about you based on things like your attire and grooming, posture, handshake (that again!), eye contact, voice, vocabulary and how you hold yourself and take up space. There's no use in lamenting how superficial this is because humans have always sized each other up based on externals. We're still Neanderthals in a lot of ways, so accept that and move on.

And then control what you can control. Audit yourself and/or solicit constructive feedback from people you trust. What impression do you make before you open your mouth? What impression do you make after you've opened your mouth? What do you say about yourself when you are saying nothing at all? And what is your personal and professional reputation? Do people think you are reliable? That you have integrity? That you are a good person? That you are flaky and noncommittal? Get all the dirt and be good enough to yourself to work on what needs working on.

Some of what you learn will be more or less relevant to what you are trying to achieve. So filter the results of your audit based on your goals and then . . .

Personal Presence: Tightening

Then it's just a matter of working on what needs working on. If you hear your grooming is letting you down, you can invest in a consultant or ask a friend to help make you over (only if this friend is well-groomed for your industry too!). If you hear that you speak too softly to be taken seriously, you can invest in a voice coach. If you don't command presence because you shrink into yourself, you can enrol in acting classes.

You don't need to throw money down the drain but do invest in what needs investing in. You can get lots of free tutorials online, where your investment is time and effort. Or you can hire specialists where your investment is money, time and effort. Audit your resources and invest what you can afford (time, money, energy) AND invest what is appropriate for what you are trying to achieve (if you are trying to become CEO of your company, it might be a good use of your resources to hire a stylist and a voice coach, for example, but if you are trying to become a YouTube cookery star, then a stylist might not be the best option for you, but free food video tutorials might be). Be careful and selective about what you invest in. Because you are investing in you, and in your Mission.

Targeted 'Leaks': Supercharging Your Visibility and Profile

Remember, you are not legally sworn to secrecy about yourself or beholden to the National Security Act. So, once you've laid the groundwork with your profiles and your personal presence is all buttoned up and looking sharp, here's where things get fun. Because it's not enough to have a message that only you put on your platforms for your existing-and-growing audience – to supercharge your visibility and your impact, you need to leverage other people's platforms and their audiences, too. Governments around the world use targeted leaks of sensitive information for strategic purposes and you can do the same as you step into the light.

Whether it's a cause you care about, a skill you want to teach or an award you want to win, the more people who see you doing your thing, the more people you tell about your Mission or message – the more people you strategically 'leak' things to – the greater your impact will be. It might take a while for the leaks to bear fruit but they always do, and sometimes in unexpected ways. And when they do bear fruit for you, you have to be ready. That's why sharpening your profiles and presence is so important. Because when your leaks hit their intended target (a recruiter, a talent scout, an event organizer, a journalist, etc.), they will search for you or ask around about you, and you want to make sure that what they see and hear is your rightest, tightest self. Not a blurry selfie and some gibberish about your hobbies. Not a reputation for sometimes coming through at the last minute or being a tactless firecracker. You at your best. You after you have worked on the things that you acknowledge need working on. This remains true no matter where you are in your career; getting to the 'top' doesn't make this stop.

Sometimes those targeted leaks will set off a chain of whispers . . . this is exactly what you want! People will start talking about you, referring others to you, following you online, subscribing to your newsletter and approaching you to do your thing. And when that happens, you will need to be ready to 'leak' yourself to this new audience. (Is it just me or is all this talk of 'leaks' getting anyone else twitchy for the toilet . . . ? Let's swap 'leak' for 'pitch' from here on, shall we?)

Getting comfortable *pitching* yourself will allow you to leverage other people's connections, audiences, networks and events, and broadcast your profile more broadly. And while it is wonderful when the trail of whispers sends the relevant audience your way, you also have to keep doing the work and keep pitching yourself again. And again. And again.

If you're running out of ideas for where and what to pitch for, put your spy skills to good use and follow the leads:

- **Pay attention to your peers/competitors**: What awards, mentions or features have they received? Look into the details and if you qualify too then throw your hat in.

- **Keep an eye out for industry conferences or events**: Which ones are relevant for you/your Mission/your message? Are they looking for speakers or workshop leaders? Do the research and then put yourself forward. You can start small with a local Meetup group, say, and then work your way up to bigger stages and audiences.

- **Research the magazines/publications/podcasts that have cachet in your field**: Find out who writes for them, edits them, hosts them and then pitch yourself as a contributor or guest. Again, you can start small with a local newspaper or radio station and work your way up to bigger readerships and audiences.

It's really that straightforward: find out what is happening and who's in charge and then **put yourself forward**. (And get comfortable with rejection. That is just part of the process; it's not a sign from the universe that you suck and should crawl into a hole.) Don't over-complicate it. Follow the leads. Create your own. And then pitch yourself. The world – and editors and conference-goers and podcast hosts and pretty much every audience that you can envision – is sick of hearing from the same voices, so add yours to the mix.

You won't always get what you want. But working through the 'no's' until you hit a 'yes' is part of the deal. And no after no, yes after yes, you will reach the people you want to reach and achieve what you want to achieve.

Remember: there is nothing holy about obscurity or anonymity. And there is nothing *un*holy about not staying obscure or anonymous. The world needs and wants to hear new and interesting perspectives from new and interesting people, and that new and interesting person is you.

So stop being squeamish and leak yourself!

Executive Order: Pitching yourself doesn't come naturally to most of us but I can say with the confidence that comes from having helped countless people – including myself – become more visible and more comfortable with pitching themselves, that you can do it and you can do it on your terms. Despite the ick-factor and the rejection factor, you can keep going because your bigger dream/goal/message requires you to do so.

So when you find yourself flagging or shrinking back into the shadows, remember: you can't help anyone – with your product, your knowledge, your insights, your service, your humour, your story – if they don't know you're there.

Do it your way and do it for them; this is not just about you.

Self-full without Becoming Full of Yourself

Here's the final thing I'll say about being more visible. For some people, there might be a slippery slope from increased visibility to obsession with fame but that is not who you are. (I know because I have eyes and ears everywhere, of course!) You are not the type of person who would go down that slide and if you are worried you might, you can use your Ops Team to rein you in.

Because here's what I know about you: you are good. You are capable. You have a voice. And you have value to share. I am a cynic about most things but not about humans. I know you are good because most people are.

So share your goodness. Use it to make your life better or other people's lives better. You have something to contribute so contribute it. There are billions of fellow humans who do not have the luxury of shining, being seen, being heard or even contemplating these things. So use the privilege you have on behalf of everyone who doesn't and shine on. Step into the fact that you can be a role model for someone else who might desperately need to see you out there. And own it.

You can do good with your goodness. More good than you might ever possibly know.

Key Intel

- Being more visible will help you achieve your goals. I repeat: being more visible will help you achieve your goals.

Stepping Out from the Shadows

- Take pride in your story; you have more to share and contribute than you probably give yourself credit for and you can uncover your 'gems' by mining yourself.
- Don't rush out into the world and start shouting indiscriminately; decide who you want to reach, how you want to reach them, what you want to share and how what you share will bring value to their lives.
- Audit and work on improving your social profiles and your personal presence/reputation; control what you can control and be open to feedback from people who are qualified to give it to you.
- Invest resources in improving what needs improving. Match your investment with your resources and your end-goal.
- Use targeted 'leaks' to pitch yourself and put yourself forward. Don't wait to be discovered. You are not Kate Moss and you are not beholden to the National Security Act, either!

Chapter 10
Developing Your Own Tradecraft

Case File: Be the Role Model You Wish You Had

When I was pregnant with my first child, I was really anxious. Not about parenthood or the baby or the pregnancy (I was lucky on all of those counts), but about what I thought I would inevitably become. I was scared that after my baby was born, people would dismiss me as 'just' a mom. I was worried that my 'baby bump' would last forever and I'd never get my fitness or muscle tone back. I was terrified that having a child and caring for it would set my career and ambitions back for good. I carried all kinds of lingering defeatism about what parenthood would mean and how it would look.

And I didn't like any of those looks.

Because I still wanted to be treated as an individual even after becoming twinned with an infant. I still wanted to be fit and toned even after becoming rounded with baby bumps and breast milk. I still wanted to tirelessly chase my dreams even after becoming tired all the time chasing after a little human.

But that seemed impossible, and I hate impossible.

So I got digging. I turned to Google. I searched for stories of women who didn't give up on themselves or on their dreams after they had kids. I looked for athletes who had become pregnant while still competing professionally. I cherry-picked examples from among my own friends and focused on moms who had multiple kids and still bossed their careers. I searched for all the evidence I could find to prove my worst anxieties wrong, to prove that there were other 'looks', as it were, that I could get down with.

And guess what? I found what I was looking for. Story after story after real-life story of real-life women (some who I knew, some who I didn't) who didn't let parenthood take over their identities, who stayed who they were, who cared about themselves and their ambitions, who had deep relationships with their partners and did a damned good job at raising damned good kids.

But then I had to prove to myself what *I* was capable of. I had learned what was possible for others, now I had to see what I could make possible for myself. So I chose to become a devoted parent and also chose to stay devoted to my career. I chose to watch my infant take her first small steady steps and also chose to take my own small steady steps to getting toned and strong again. I made time for my amazing daughter and I made time for my amazing self. I created one-on-one memories with my baby and I created one-on-one memories with my man.

I didn't give up on myself. I didn't give in to impossible. I became the person I wanted to become – a loving parent who also loved herself, someone who cherished the new life she had created and also cherished her own life – and became the role model I had been looking for all along. By making choices. And by asking for help so I could make those choices.

Because that is what life requires of us all. There will be times when you look for role models and can't find one that ticks all the boxes. When you search and search, and the world turns up crumbs. When you'll look outward to no avail and are forced to look inward to prevail. And you will have to choose and chart your own way.

Being your own role model doesn't mean going it alone. It will require – demand – that you get support. Ask for help. Lean on others along the way. This doesn't make you weak, it makes you real.

Roger Bannister didn't let a lack of role models stop him from becoming the first person to run a four-minute mile; he chose to eschew 'impossible' and became a role model for himself – while relying on two other runners to keep his pace; he couldn't have become a first without them. Madam C J Walker didn't let a lack of role models keep her from becoming the first self-made woman (and first Black woman) millionaire in America; she chose to eschew 'impossible', and massive racial and social barriers to boot, and became a role model for herself – while relying on an army of 25,000 sales agents to help her business flourish; she couldn't have become a first without them.

Their greatness was never a solo flight but it was an uncharted one.

So when your path is uncharted and uncertain, when there is no one out there to show you, when you can't 'see it to be it', remember that sometimes *you* have to be it so that others can see it. We all have that power. And being bolder requires us to recognize and unleash that power. For others, of course, but first and foremost for ourselves.

One of the many life-expanding things about working at the CIA was that I got to work with some exceptional be-it-so-others-can-see-it role models and internalize the powerful make-shit-happen ethos that pervaded our organization. I once had a boss who advised me that 'it's better to beg for forgiveness than ask for permission'. Subtext: play within the rules but play with how far you can stretch them.

Before I joined the CIA, though, I was familiar with the idea of be-it-so-others-can-see-it role models and make-shit-happen power, as both were very much a part of our family. My mother often told me that as a woman and person of colour, I would have to work at least twice as hard as my white or male counterparts, but that was never an excuse to stop or give up. Subtext: know what you're up against but don't let other people's bullshit stop you. (This is the same woman who left her group medical practice when she was in her late fifties – yes, fifties! – and started her own private practice. Talk about being unstoppable.)

So when I made the transition into starting my own businesses, unshakable persistence and expansive notions of what we can all make possible for ourselves were hard-wired into me. But I had yet to prove to myself what I could do in a business context, so I adapted those lessons. I used the anvil of all of my life experiences to forge new tools, to create my own tradecraft, to devise my own techniques and methods for pursuing my Mission.

And you can, too. In the pages ahead, I'll be walking you through how to develop your tradecraft – your own techniques and methods for pursuing your Mission – just as I have done and helped others to do. I'll show you how to rewrite the rules, utilize your full arsenal and create the tools you need for whatever your Mission may be.

Rewriting the 'Rules'

Here's some irony for you: I am a total rule follower. I like neatness. And order. And even when I'm being carefree, I am pretty careful (there's a story my sister loves to tell about my 18-year-old self being mindlessly drunk at a house party she was throwing but I was still mindful enough to hook a plastic bag around my ears so I didn't throw up on her bedroom floor!). But I also think a lot of rules – and their trenchant cousins, social conventions – are stupid. I crawl under the rope barriers at airports when there is no one in the line (much to the horror of my English husband!). I eat with my left hand (much to the horror of my grandmother!). I sit with the men. I ask for exceptions. Or I make them for myself.

I'm not an anarchist – nor am I advocating it – but I have been endowed with a brain, and I like to use it to question the way things are done to see if there is a better way. And you can, too. In fact, I very much recommend that you do. We have done so much work together on unpicking assumptions, questioning sources and interrogating intel, so let's take it up a notch and see how you can bend, stretch or rewrite the social conventions that are keeping you from being your biggest, best, boldest self.

First principles – Indulge the Whys

My dad is a surgeon by training but an engineer by temperament. He has always encouraged us to master and truly understand the principles, the foundations, the basics of anything we do so we can make sensible decisions about everything that is built upon them. From money management to building houses, this 'first principles' training has been invaluable because it has given me a grounding in investigating and asking 'why?' until I get to the reason behind things and until I truly understand.

I have also been blessed with a daughter who reminds me daily of first principles (for anyone with a toddler in your life, you will appreciate what I'm about to share) because at any given moment, in any given scenario, she never fails to ask 'Why?' And then keeps asking it until she is satisfied, until she truly understands.

'Why do I have to go to bed?' 'Because it's bedtime.' *'Why is it bedtime?'* 'Because at the end of the day, we go to sleep so our brains and bodies can rest.' *'Why do we need to rest?'* 'Because when we learn things and do things every day we use energy so we need to rest to get energy back.' *'Why do we learn things?'* 'Because life is all about learning and doing.' *'Why?'* 'Because otherwise it would be boring, and we would be boring.' *'Why?'* . . . And we keep going and going, no matter how long it takes, until she is satisfied, until she truly understands.

And this first-principles, 'why?' approach to the 'given' world is incredibly useful for all of us – in life, in business, in everything – because whys taken to their logical conclusions can be powerfully illuminating.

A few years ago, I was mired in a frustrating battle with my Instagram account (I couldn't figure out how to use it!)

and I caught myself wondering, *'Why the hell am I doing this?'* And then I found myself playing the why-game. *'Because I ended the contract with my social media person for sucking.'* Why? *'Because I trusted her blindly and was rewarded with mediocrity.'* Why? *'Because I was so glad to not be doing social media that I didn't check up on her and forgot that delegation is not abdication.'* Why? *'Because you can trust people but need to verify your trust . . .'*

And from that exchange with myself, I re-remembered lessons about management, accountability and ownership. I remembered that just because one person let me down, that doesn't mean everyone will. So I then asked my amazing VA to help me with the social media stuff and since then have found another social media company to help. That small ah-ha, why-driven change (re-delegating something I am not uniquely qualified to do and not giving up on asking for help) would never have happened had I kept my 'Why the hell . . . ?' question rhetorical.

Every time you get frustrated, every time you ask yourself 'why is this so?', or 'why is that not so?', it is an opportunity to uncover something, to get back to first principles and then act on those principles. So don't keep it rhetorical.

Do you think your business needs to grow this year? Why? Do you think you need to hire more staff? Why? Do you think you need to start posting on Facebook to get clients? Why? Do you think you need to consider a different investment strategy? Why? Do you think you need to change careers? Why? Do you think you can't fulfil your dreams? Why?

Indulge the whys . . .

Is there a better way?

. . . And then once you get to the bottom of things, once you get to the first principles, then you can decide what to do. If the principles are sound, great; you can change your approach if needed. And if the principles are not sound, equally great; you can challenge the principles.

Here's an example: after my first daughter was born, I was still running my business full-time. And I remember worrying about – as I shared above – how to do both things well: boss my career and be a good parent. I had assumed that I would have to separate my work life from my mother-hood life but that wasn't an option. There was one me and two demands. So I got down to first principles. The reason *why* I thought I had to separate my work from my motherhood was because of stupid social conventions that said so, that kept dividing 'work' from 'life'. But that was not a principle I thought was very sound. So I challenged it.

I brought my infant daughter to investor meetings without asking or apologizing. I breastfed her while on the phone with partners without asking or apologizing. I took her to events where I was the speaker without asking or apologizing. My husband brought her to events where I was the host without asking or apologizing. I challenged the principle and rewrote the unspoken rules about having to keep the different parts of my life always separate.

And then I rewrote the rules for others who might not have known they could do it for themselves. At the business events I hosted, I stood at the front of the room and told all the parents there (not just the women) that their kids were welcome to come with them. That they didn't have to choose between being parents and being professionals. That 'work–life' separation was confusing bullshit because work *is* part of life. Life requires work. And the guests at my events brought their kids. Not all the time. But if and when they needed or wanted to.

We rewrote rules that were based on faulty principles.

Another example: women are still told too often that pregnancy should be treated like an illness, that we are in a 'delicate' state so should put our feet up, eat for two and move as little as possible. What a stupid, infantilizing way to treat bodies that are powerful enough to create life. To. Create. Life.

So I challenged the 'rules'. I asked all the whys in the world and found that the principles were unsound . . . and then I used common sense. Women have been birthing for millennia while having an active and physical role to play in hunting and gathering. The women in my own family kept working on farms and gave birth at home without the benefits of modern medicine. The stay-sedentary-and-do-nothing principle didn't apply to all women and it sure as shit didn't apply to me, as a healthy woman who had an uncomplicated pregnancy.

So I kept exercising. I stayed active. I never stopped working. I was in the gym – doing modified workouts, but still in the gym – three days before my first daughter was born. And I was doing push ups two weeks before my second daughter was. I rewrote the rules that didn't apply to me and that were based on somewhat chauvinistic, women-are-the-weaker-sex principles. And in doing so, I rewrote the rules for others. I had a number of women come up to me at the gym and tell me that they saw me working out while heavily pregnant and that inspired them to do the same, after they confirmed with their doctors and trainers what they could and couldn't do.

So my friends, don't take anything for granted. Any-thing that is keeping you small or frustrated or in conflict with yourself can be questioned. Indulge the whys, let them lead you logically to first principles. And then challenge or change or ignore what needs to be challenged or changed or ignored.

Everything is 'impossible' until someone does it. And that someone who rewrites 'impossible' into 'possible' can be you.

Developing Your Own Tradecraft

Use Your Full Arsenal

Rewriting 'impossible' into 'possible' and developing your own tradecraft will also require you to make use of your full arsenal of skills, attributes, identities and everything that comes with them, as well as the All-Source Intel you've picked up along your life's journey. Don't take any of what you have for granted or leave it to collect dust. Let's dive in and do a full inventory of all you have to work with so you can polish it and put it to good use in new ways.

Your Personal Arsenal

When I was serving in a war zone, my radio call sign was Arsenal, in honour of the Premier League team made great by the great Arsène Wenger. I had naively assumed anyone who heard me use it in the field would strike up a conversation about favourite players (Dennis Bergkamp, if you want to know) and memorable fixtures (October 2002 against Everton when Wayne Rooney ended our unbeaten streak and February 2010 against Stoke when Ryan Shawcross broke Aaron Ramsey's leg . . . the image of that dangling tibia will stay seared in my brain forever). But sadly, there weren't many fellow Gooners in the badlands and the only time it came up was when one of the security guys asked me if I had chosen my call sign because, he said, with a literal smack of his lips, I had 'the full arsenal'.

Now, vomit-inducing pick-up lines aside, using your 'full arsenal' is a valuable life lesson that too many of us forget. Rarely do we do a pen-to-paper review of ourselves and our assets. We forget. We take for granted. We think what is ours is normal. And we fail to appreciate the full extent of what we've got. But no more! You are analyzing everything, rewriting rules, developing tradecraft and heading for heights. And you are going to need everything that is within your reach to do it. So let's get looking at all of the 'weapons' you've got in your personal arsenal, including your:

- **Intellectual arsenal:** what you can do, what you have learned, your mindset

- **Social arsenal:** who you know, your standing, your reputation, your influence

- **Familial arsenal:** family connections, emotional support, practical support

- **Financial arsenal**: what you currently have, earn or own

- **Interpersonal arsenal**: your networks and extended relationships

- **Physical arsenal**: your capabilities and appearance

- **Reputational arsenal**: what people say about you and what your life story says about you

Developing Your Own Tradecraft

Not all of these arsenals will be equally endowed and that's what makes it fun: you will be forced to use creativity and ingenuity to put your mix of weapons to use in the way that makes best use of them. You can sharpen what's there and try to forge new tools from what you have to make up for any gaps if you need to.

But first you have to know what you're working with. So sit down, get thinking, and write down all of the assets that will help you achieve what you want to achieve, be who you want to be, do what you want to do and have what you want to have. Now make note of the 'weapons' that are worn from overuse and which ones are dusty from neglect. Switch things up and use them all.

I'm not saying that you should use the tools you have to get anything you don't deserve, but you should definitely use all of the tools you have to get what you *do* deserve and achieve the things you are capable of achieving.

It is a myth that we live in a meritocracy – no matter where you live or where you work, this is true. There isn't someone out there watching and waiting to reward you when you 'deserve' it (if you still think so, please re-read Chapter 9). So:

If you have social connections that will get your resume in front of the right eyes, use those connections to get your resume in front of the right eyes.

If you have family backing that can help you start your new business, make use of that backing.

If you have a beaming smile that can get you better customer service, turn up the wattage.

If you have a unique life experience that can get you elected into office, make sure everyone knows about that life experience.

Use all of the gifts you have, instead of pretending you only have a few.

An elite athlete would never stunt their professional career by playing down their other assets like charm or good looks, and neither should you.

An agent in the field would never hamstring themselves by leaving behind their persuasion skills or self-defence powers, and neither should you.

A CEO would never dial down their deal-closing prowess or interpersonal magnetism, and neither should you.

Use everything you've got. Use your full arsenal because there is no moral hierarchy to the tools and endowments you are gifted with. They are just tools. And like all tools, they can be used for good or for bad. So use yours for good, with integrity, and move on.

Your All-Source Intel

The other part of your arsenal that you should use to develop your own tradecraft is the All-Source Intel – the wisdom, experience and lessons you have received from family, culture, heritage, hobbies, books, podcasts, history, science, art, aphorisms – all of the richness of human learning you have come across and bathed in since birth. Remember it, draw on it and use it in your own way and for your own Mission. And keep adding to it. Pay attention when people say interesting things, go to the library and browse different sections, listen to a lecture on YouTube, watch a TED Talk, keep your eyes and ears open, write ideas down. Be an information magpie: collect a bit of this, a bit of that, and then sit down and think about how you can use it in pursuit of your goals.

When I was a child, my dad used to enlist me to help with his office admin, which for doctors is never-ending. I was tasked with folding letters just so, putting them in envelopes, affixing postage stamps and making sure the address in the letter was the same as on the envelope. It was boring and repetitive but I learned an important lesson about efficiency. My dad showed me how to thoughtfully lay everything out on the kitchen table and do things in a particular order and in small batches so that my production line minimized wasted movement, maximized the benefits of batching and allowed for small improvements to be made without experimenting on the whole. And now, whenever I am doing any menial or repetitive or admin task, guess what? I use my dad's method to plan, set up, minimize wasted effort and batch. All that boredom and eye-rolling as a kid paid off in hours (and hours!) and resources saved as an adult who runs her own businesses. Who knew?

More recently, my cousin was cooking me dinner and said the phrase *mise-en-place* in passing. I had never heard it before, so asked her to explain. It essentially means chopping all of your ingredients and laying out all the gear you need to prepare your meal before you start to cook. This way, no time is wasted hunting for anything – or realizing too late you are missing an ingredient – and the cooking process becomes seamless and frustration-free. But since I don't cook, I tried to think of how I could use the same interesting principle – get everything ready before you start – the same intel, in a business context. And I did. I now *mise-en-place* all of my business projects by lining up all of the supporting team I will need, laying out all of the different tasks for the project, making sure each task has someone leading it and outlining the order in which each person has to throw their lot into the metaphorical frying pan. Only after everything is prepped and ready to go do we start 'cooking' and the project launch and delivery process becomes just as straightforward and fuss-free as my cousin's meals.

This is what I mean by using your All-Source Intel to create your own tradecraft. Your life is awash with useful insights but you need to look out for them, adapt them and then use them. Not all of your intel can be used in every context but every bit can be used in *a* context. I don't try to weave my amateurish love for astrophysics into my fitness routine, for example, but I do bring the sense of wonder I get from reading Neil deGrasse Tyson into my daily appreciation-for-life routine.

We all have many intel streams feeding into our lives, so take time to pay attention to yours and let them help you be bigger, better and bolder than you ever thought possible.

If It Doesn't Exist, Create It

Developing your own tradecraft for how to live, lead and succeed will require you to get used to the idea that you can be the source of (almost) everything you need, whether that means being your own role model from time to time or creating the tools you need.

When I was at the CIA, I forged new partnerships to better serve our Mission. When I was in business school, I hosted salons to better serve my hungry right-brain. When I became an entrepreneur, I created a community for women founders to better serve others. In each instance, I noticed a lack and I filled the gap. And you, of course, can do the same.

By now, through all of the work we have done together, you have rediscovered your own power, your own skills, your own assets, your own arsenal and perhaps you are getting bored of me telling you how capable you are. Good. Because I want you to be so well-versed in your own amazingness that it becomes mundane and acknowledged, but no longer ignored.

Whatever it is you strive for, use your full arsenal to rewrite what needs rewriting, build what needs building and do what needs doing.

Because you can.

Key Intel

- Rewrite the rules and social conventions that are holding you back. Just because something is 'the done thing' doesn't mean there is a good reason for it being so!

- Indulge the whys behind what you think is/isn't possible and get back to first principles; once you understand what's at the bottom of the 'why' you can decide if the principle needs correcting. If so, correct it by identifying a new/better way to operate.

- Make use of your full arsenal: the intellectual, social, familial, financial, interpersonal, physical and reputational 'weapons' within your reach. There is no moral hierarchy inherent in any of these tools; it's how you use the tools that gives them a moral weight.

- Your arsenal also includes the All-Source Intel that you have been bathing in since birth. Draw on it and use it in new ways.

- Use all of your knowledge and assets to develop your own unique tradecraft tools that serve you and your Mission best.

- You can be the one to change 'impossible' into 'possible' for yourself. Use everything you've got to do just that.

Chapter 11
Tactical Ignorance

Case File: Ready for Battle

When I did my war zone service, a large part of my role was to brief the commanding general of US and international forces on the Agency's most up-to-date analysis of the war effort. My position was unique because as a civilian I was outside of the military hierarchy. So even though what I was sharing with the general was high-stakes stuff, my career didn't depend on keeping him happy. It was still an awkward role, though, going in every day with mostly brutal honesty, and I chose not to make it even more awkward by psyching myself out and obsessing over how 'important' he was (he was a four-star general after all) compared to how 'lowly' I was (I was 26 and relatively early in my career at the time). I kept the noise about status and hierarchy where it belonged: on a street called 'Nowhere' in a town called 'Near Me'.

When you are working in an active battle arena, it's hard not to get wrapped up in ranks and who sits where. But doing so would not have helped me do my job. So I tactically managed the information I took in and the information I ignored. I retained what was relevant (the intelligence analysis and why the general needed to know it) and dismissed the irrelevant (the 'importance' of the person I was talking to). And by doing this, I was able to keep myself together.

I didn't freak out when the general questioned me; it was just a question from a person. I didn't crawl under the table when the general disagreed with me – on more than one occasion our analysis diverged significantly from what he had been told by his own intelligence officers; hearing, 'That's not what I've heard from my Commanders,' was more inner-steel-testing than any red-hot forge! – it was just a disagreement from a person (and a disagreement it was my job to then counter with facts and proof). And I didn't worry about who was looking at who around the table; they were just people looking at each other and if they chose not to verbalize what they were thinking then it wasn't my business to agonize about it.

I focused on the job, not on the noise.

This isn't to say I blundered in and bull-in-a-china-shop'ed my way through. Of course I was respectful. The man had earned four stars, and that deserves respect. I called him 'Sir' or 'General' and acknowledged his status, but I didn't let that status make me insignificant. I had a job, a critical task. And while we most definitely weren't equals in rank, we sure as shit were equals in being in the fight together. So I acknowledged my equality, too.

This is the thing we have to remember: everyone is equal. We may not all be equally gifted or equally lucky or equally smart or equally anything, but we are equally human. And we can choose to focus on where we are equal with someone else – and get on with our lives and our jobs – or obsess over where we are unequal – and lock ourselves in mentally subservient positions.

So remember that the next time you are in a room wondering if you belong there. You do. You might have fought your way in or been invited. It doesn't matter. But once you're in there, act like you belong there – because you do – and get the job done.

I developed Tactical Ignorance when I was working in a war zone but it has served me incredibly well in everything I have done since, professionally and personally. What makes it so powerful is the 'tactical' part. I would never advocate burying our heads in the sand about anything (that's not very boss-like) but I am a huge advocate for being strategic about the inputs we let in.

As a former analyst who regularly parsed huge amounts of data, of course I have a reverence for research. But as a CEO who has also now worked with hundreds of other leaders and creators, I've seen the 'dark side' of data, too, and how too much information can arrest growth, progress and creativity, and silence intuition. That's why we need to *curate* our ignorance and consciously choose the inputs we will *not* pay attention to – that is, be tactical about it – because in doing so, we can find the confidence and creativity required to get out of our own way. Not all information is worth having and a certain level of deliberate ignorance can free us from the shackles of precedent, and stop us from killing our ideas and Missions before they are born.

In the pages ahead, we'll be looking at how you can powerfully 'under'-prepare, thrive on a low-info diet and use plausible deniability (a.k.a. not asking questions you don't want the answers to) to achieve what you want to achieve. Consider this your tactical ignorance basic training.

The Power of 'Under'-preparing

A few years ago a friend of mine casually suggested that I should host a podcast. He and I had become friends after he had interviewed me for his podcast, and he thought I had the skills to be a good host myself. So I decided to give it a go. I chose to focus on stories of women founders (to give more of them a chance to step out of the shadows) and found my first season's worth of interviewees through my various networks.

At this point, I could have gone into overdrive looking at how other hosts conducted their interviews, making lists of best practices and styles, and wasting time 'preparing' by listening to every other podcast out there about or for women founders to make sure mine was as uniquely niche-y as it possibly could be. But I didn't. That wasn't the job. The job was to host *my* podcast, not other people's, so I tactically ignored all of the comparisonitis-masked-as-research noise and consciously chose to host my podcast my way.

Then when I started to record the interviews, I had to make a similar choice. I could have googled each guest to death and made sure I knew every bit of their life's story from first breath to most recent bowel movement, but I didn't. I chose to learn just enough to get the conversation going – and not be an ignoramus! – but not so much that even I would be bored because I already knew everything there was to know about them. I focused on the job: to have an interesting conversation that was honest and insightful and I tactically ignored the pull to research my guests into oblivion.

And guess what? To this day, I have interviewed over 60 founders and counting and not one of those conversations has been boring. Not one of those conversations was stultified by scripts or punctured by prepared remarks. They were casual, free-wheeling, interesting and natural. We talked like normal people talk and by 'under'-preparing, I was able to be genuinely interested in their answers, to let the conversation go to unexpected but illuminating places.

Everyone enjoyed the result far more than if I had run through a series of pre-rehearsed questions.

But I was also a considerate host. If my guests wanted to prepare, I gave them broad, open-ended questions to consider in advance and allowed them to prepare how they wanted to. Just because I was 'under'-preparing, didn't mean they had to. But we worked together, their style and my own, and I have loved and learned from each conversation because of it.

Not letting myself get stuck in the preparation also allowed me to have an actual podcast instead of a podcast *idea*. I got started with just enough information and 'under'-prepared by doing the recordings before I knew how to broadcast them. And then I figured out the technical bits (RSS feeds, hosting platforms, etc.) along the way.

Too many people keep themselves from doing something because they feel they aren't ready yet. They hide behind information gathering, or degree gathering, or qualification gathering so that someone else can tell them when they are prepared enough. But that (you can anticipate it coming) is total horseshit. You can get started with 'enough' right now, with whatever you already have, figure the rest out later and learn more as you go. Poring over data and minutiae is not the same as doing. It's procrasti-preparing and you are hiding behind it.

If you want to push back on a recent board decision about executive compensation, don't get bogged down in the details of compensation regulation and precedence. Focus on having enough conversations with individual board members so you can understand their rationale and then get counter-arguing.

If you want to present your brilliant marketing ideas to your company's leadership team, don't get bogged down in researching every last detail about every previous marketing campaign and tell yourself you have to write a comparative thesis on the evolution of marketing best practice before you are smart enough to present anything (you laugh, but I see you, Over-deliverers Anonymous!). Focus on gathering enough marketing stats to get going and then get presenting.

If you want to pitch your start-up idea to a room full of investors, don't get bogged down in the minutiae of each investor's portfolio investments and do a point-for-point analysis about how your venture is better. Focus on gathering enough data about their investment trends and patterns to inform your expectations and presentation, and then get pitching.

If you want to become MD of your company, don't get bogged down agonizing over whether you should get an MBA or a finance degree or if you could get a leadership certification instead or look for some other form of procrasti-training. Focus on the actual job spec, work on building enough of the identified skills and then apply for the job.

That's it. That's the trick. Do enough to get started and then start.

Thriving on a Low-info Diet

The other way you can use tactical ignorance to get out of your own way is to subsist on a low-info diet. Not no info, low info. Info that is tactically and strategically chosen.

When I was pregnant the first time, I once (and only once) made the mistake of googling something about 'geriatric pregnancies' because at the ripe old age of 36, I was already branded a 'geriatric mom'. It only took a perusal of the first two scare-mongering 'hits' before I literally closed my computer. I couldn't change the fact that I was 36, so I decided I was not going to obsess about the alleged risks of being 'old'. I knew my body. I knew how healthy I was. And I generally knew what the risks were but I didn't go looking for things to worry about. I decided to trust my own good sense, trust the power of my body (backed up by millennia of women giving birth without Google at their side) and trust my appointments with my midwife.

I *chose* the low info I took in: what foods I could/couldn't eat, what types of exercise the professionals who knew me told me I could/couldn't do, and I trusted my intuition. If something didn't feel right or sound right, I questioned it. But I didn't let myself get sucked into the black hole of the internet, turn into a worry-filled wreck and ruin my pregnancy to boot!

The same happened when I started my first business. Sure, I could have endlessly researched the risks of becoming an entrepreneur but everything in life comes with some risk. So I simply spoke to people who had experience starting and scaling businesses in the same industry; I read credible journals and used my common sense to analyze the information and I trusted my intuition. I questioned what I needed to question but I didn't let myself turn into a worry-filled wreck who never started a business because it was too risky.

We all have to do that. We all have to choose which information we will consume and which we will spit back out or not put on our plates at all. Not all information is worth having, not all information is created equal and not all information is informative.

In the heady days of the first Covid lockdown, I stopped watching the 'news' because all it did was say the same thing day after day. And while the statistics of cases and deaths were harrowing, I didn't need to know the precise numbers because I had zero control over them. And filling my head with information about things I cannot control is a huge waste of time, energy and emotion. I don't have nearly enough of those things to spare and I'm pretty sure you don't either.

So tune into yourself. Tune into your goals. Tune into your intuition and your Situational Awareness and decide what information you need and what 'information' is just a distraction or not informative at all. And then ignore all of the information that is not directly relevant to what you care about or what you want to achieve. Slash and burn your way through your email subscriptions, WhatsApp groups, Instagram feeds, radio stations, podcast lists – all of the inputs you mindlessly consume – and recognize that each input is either lifting you higher or pulling you backward. There is no stasis.

You are what you eat, after all, and that is just as true of your information diet as it is of your gastronomic one.

> **Executive Order:** What I'm about to executive order you to do might sound harsh and puritanical if you've never thought about all the noise coming at you all day long but people, my people, our brains are powerful and pick up far more subconsciously than we are consciously aware of (self-evident from the word 'subconscious', I know). And that's why our inputs are so important. Because whether we register them or not, they are being processed. And like the work we did in the SA exercises in Part One, our inputs will have an impact on our outputs. It's not magic, it's science.
>
> So choose your inputs. Be conscious of them. If you are around negative people all the time, you are likely to be more negative. If all you read is romance

fluff, your world view will be more fluffy. If you listen to angry podcasters, you'll internalize some of their anger. It's easy to dismiss these things as 'small stuff' but they are not small. Everything leaves an imprint.

Be aware of what you are taking in and create boundaries around how much negativity, fluff or anger you let in. Because if you have big goals, big dreams, big anything – and I know you do or you wouldn't have made it this far – then you will need to make some big shifts in the way you think, lead and live. As Einstein famously said, doing the same thing over and over and expecting different results is insanity.

So stop doing the same thing. Stop expecting your outputs to change if you're not changing your inputs. It all matters – to different degrees, sure, but it all matters. Don't dismiss the small stuff. It can have a big impact on where you go and how long it takes you to get there.

Plausible Deniability

When I was living in New York in my twenties, my then-boyfriend and I were regulars on the Sunday nightclub scene. The Meatpacking district was the place to be and Lotus was its epicentre. It was there that I literally ran into Lenny Kravitz (swoon!) and there that my boyfriend had drinks with David Copperfield and Salman Rushdie.

As any nightclub goer knows, there are subtle, often Byzantine, rules to getting in. And rule number one is you never, never go up to the person on the door and ask, 'Can I get in?'

Never.

This is also true for much of life beyond the velvet rope.

Questions are powerful things, you see, because too often we let the answer determine the outcome. And asking the question to begin with gives all the power to the person we are asking. But you can choose to not ask. You can choose to determine the outcome yourself. You can choose to retain the power for yourself.

So don't ask:

- Questions you know will be met with a 'no', or
- Questions that you intuitively know the answers to, and those answers scare, subdue or silence you

That is being tactically ignorant.

Because if you don't ask the question, you can always hide behind plausible deniability – a classic CIA move! *'Oh my,'* Rosa Parks smiled knowingly to herself as she ignited a movement, *'I can't sit here . . . ?'*

'Civil disobedience isn't the done thing?' snickered Gandhi to himself in the face of the British Empire as he brought it to its knees. *'I had no idea, my good sirs.'*

Tactical Ignorance

That is the power of not asking questions that you know will get a no, that you don't really want the answers to because you already know the answer: you don't wait for permission to be withheld (it is already being withheld); you act and give the world a *fait accompli*. Pure. Genius.

And as for those questions that you know will return scary, subduing or silencing answers? Choose not to ask those either. When you know the odds are stacked against you, is it really worth knowing how high and mighty and intricately carved the stack? All that 'knowledge' will just give you an excuse to back down before you get started.

So don't ask questions like 'how many women become CEOs of Fortune 500 companies?'; use tactical ignorance (and the Art of the Possible, coming at you in a few pages) and all of the tools you've picked up so far to be another exception, and then help others become exceptions too.

Don't ask questions like 'how many trans people of colour have started successful funds?'; use tactical ignorance (and the Art of the Possible) and all of the tools you've picked up so far to be an exception, and help others become exceptions too.

Don't ask questions like 'how old do I have to be to start dancing/boxing/publishing?'; use tactical ignorance (and the Art of the Possible) and all of the tools you've picked up so far to be an exception, and help others become exceptions too.

Don't ask. And be tactical about it.

Use your arsenal. Use your tradecraft. Use plausible deniability. Use everything you've got to get out of your own way and into the metaphorical night club. Lenny Kravitz might just be waiting for you.

Key Intel

- Tactical ignorance is so powerful because of the 'tactical' part; you are choosing carefully what to let in and what to ignore based on your Mission at hand.
- Part of being tactical means also getting comfortable with 'under'-preparing because it forces you to start with enough instead of procrasti-training or procrasti-learning.
- You know yourself well enough to know what effect all of the various inputs coming your way have on you, so cut out the garbage and curate your low-info diet.
- Plausible deniability is your friend; choose what not to ask and just make things happen.

Chapter 12
Unshakable

Case File: The Pursuit of Aliveness

Soon after I gave birth to our second daughter, I was having a conversation with my doula that turned philosophical (big life changes have a way of bringing out my inner Socrates). We were talking about how here in the West, we have become so accustomed to easy lives of comfort that we feel entitled to happiness and chase it obsessively (it's even enshrined in the US Declaration of Independence as an unalienable right). We hide from pain, avoid discomfort, rush through difficulty, try to wish away anything that feels awkward.

But what if we let go of the pursuit of happiness and chased something deeper instead? What if we traded happiness for alive-ness?

We all know happiness can be elusive. And the world doesn't owe us anything. Reality takes liberties with our dreams. Life doesn't conform to our plans. And over and over, because that is just how it is, we face setbacks and challenges, choppy waters and all manner of things that don't go our way.

But truly feeling the feels, letting it be OK when things are not OK, accepting the downs with the ups – that is being alive. And by choosing to embrace aliveness, we can find meaning in the things that make us unhappy and infuse even the hardest times in our lives with purpose and energy. And we can let ourselves experience the toughness – learn from it, grow from it, become more resilient as a result of it – instead of always rushing to escape from it.

By embracing aliveness – and all the good, bad and ugly that comes with it – we can find power and strength in ourselves that we may not have known was there if we had only ever forced the happiness agenda. And we can learn how truly unshakable we are.

My dear, dear reader. We are getting close to the end of our time together and I have saved some particularly glittering gems for last. These are the tools and tactics that I have developed and honed – at the CIA, as a CEO, as a daughter of immigrants, as an Indian-American, as a parent, as an individual with my unique identity and personas – that have collectively made me pretty damned unshakable.

Sure, I get scared. Sure, I get overwhelmed. Sure, I get tired. Like everyone, I get frustrated and deflated and rejected. But I never, never, never let the fear, overwhelm, tiredness, frustration, deflation or rejection shake me. Not for long. And it sure as hell doesn't stop me.

Why not? Because I have thick skin, I have learned to trust my own power, I harness the power of being 'the only', I make things happen and I am a damned devoted practitioner of the Art of the Possible. And these are my final gifts to you. The last bit of tradecraft, a final few tools to round out your arsenal. And to leave you stirred but not shaken.

Toughen Up

When I was growing up, whenever my siblings and I came home with less than 100 per cent on a test, even if it was a 98, my parents would ask, 'What happened to the other two points?' The wonderful, if infuriating, thing about having parents who expected 100 per cent from us all the time wasn't the overplayed, 'Oh, it's so hard being me and my best is never good enough.' It was, 'Wow, my parents think I am capable of more and maybe they're right.' That was the subtext. Not oppressive perfectionism but an internalisation that people who loved me deeply thought I was capable of more than I might have realized and were helping me set my own standards higher.

So I learned to set my standards higher. And I always looked for ways to get better, faster, smarter no matter how good I was. Thanks to my parents, constructive criticism – and that is the key word here: constructive – has become my companion, feedback my friend.

So now I ask you: what happened to your other two points? Are you setting your standards high enough? And are you letting yourself down by ignoring potentially helpful feedback?

When I was a fresh-faced recruit at the Agency, I remember being so excited to share my first draft analytical report with a senior analyst for review. I thought I had done a good job and was expecting some minor comments and a heap of praise, not the blood-red-with-edits paper I got back. I was shocked. I am smart and I am thorough, and my ego was not used to less-than-stellar professional feedback. But I didn't huff into the senior analyst's office and tell him he was wrong or bitch about him to all of my friends. I read his comments, took them in, fixed what needed fixing and – here's the key – made my report better.

It wasn't personal. The senior analyst wasn't saying that I sucked as a human being and was a waste of good cubicle space; he was just saying that my report sucked. And there is a huge difference between the two: my worthiness as a human (as for all of us) is self evident; the worthiness of my report is not. And that's how you can choose to take feedback, too. Not as a commentary on you but as a mere commentary on your performance on one discrete thing.

Feedback can make us better. And we can get better at depersonalizing feedback even from sources we despise or who despise us.

In the war zone, I had a colleague who decided she didn't like me and wasted no opportunity to criticize me in the guise of offering 'friendly advice'. And every time she did, I forced myself – through gritted teeth – to divorce the substance from the source and took the advice that would make me a better analyst and officer. I didn't like it when she was right but I accepted it when she was and let her verbal swords sharpen my own arsenal. And that is the approach we all have to take. Not blindly agreeing with everything everyone says about us or our work. But hearing it, reflecting on it and then having the humility and generosity to improve what can be improved, regardless of how much we like the source, and as long as that source is qualified.

A senior analyst at the Agency who has been working there for decades is qualified to give me feedback, and I should take it; a fellow-analyst who is just as green as I am and who has no track record of being good at their job is not. A colleague who has done multiple war zone tours is qualified to give me feedback, and I should take it (even if she is nasty about it); a colleague in headquarters who has no experience in the field is not (even if they are nice about it). The same is true in our personal lives. My ultra-fit husband is qualified to tell me when I should be exercising more; my couch-potato friends are not. I will welcome feedback and advice from the former and ignore friendly compliments of how I'm 'healthy enough' from the latter.

We can all be better in some way and in order to get better, in order to see what we are capable of, we need to make feedback from people who know more about a topic than we do or have done what we want to do successfully our friend, even if the person is unfriendly. The reality of life is that no one is obligated to like us or agree with us or tell us we are great. I repeat: no one is obligated to like us or agree with us or tell us we are great. So when we do come across anything less than blind adoration, we have to let that be OK. We have to be tough enough to learn from it instead of being destroyed by it and not let our egos keep our skin paper thin and our standards painfully low.

The Power of Being the 'Only'

Just as we can choose to reframe hard-to-hear constructive feedback as an opportunity to get better and become tougher, we can also reframe being the 'only' as an opportunity to reset the agenda instead of always carrying it as a burden.

Look, being the only anything is usually pretty hard. The only woman. The only American. The only person of colour. The only civilian. The only whatever. It can come with massive pressures and crushing expectations. You are not allowed to be an individual. You become an (unwilling) representative of a whole group of people. And everything you do is hyper-scrutinized. When you do something well, it is taken for granted. But when you mess up, it becomes a symptom of your identity, a flaw inherent in everyone else who shares that identifier with you. And then that mess-up is used as an excuse to not hire or rely on or trust or work with people 'like you' again. You have to be superlative – like my mom always said – because if you aren't then no one else 'like you' will be given a chance again. Sometimes the fears and pressures we carry are just in our heads, sure, but sometimes they are all too real.

So, like I said, being the 'only' can be pretty daunting. But it can also be great. It can also be a wonderful opportunity. Because being the 'only' means we stand out. And we can use our standing out to challenge conceptions of what people 'like us' are like, move the world forward and inspire or change others for the better.

Many years ago, I was riding the bus in an English suburb quietly reading the *Economist*. The old white man sitting next to me kept peering over my shoulder so I finally tipped the magazine toward him to give his neck a break. He laughed and asked me what I was reading. I told him, with a not-so-hidden 'duh' in my voice, what it was and to my surprise he still asked, 'What's that?' (sigh). I explained that it was a political and current affairs magazine, and then it was his turn to be visibly surprised. 'Oh! It's not religious,' he said. 'I assumed someone like you would be reading about religion.'

Now, feel free to read all the subtext in the world into this conversation that you like because I sure as hell did. And my first instinct was of course to roll my eyes, be mildly offended and further dismiss this person who had no idea what the *Economist* was (for goodness' sake!). But I chose to turn my instinct on its head. If I was the only Asian-ancestored brown person this man had ever engaged in a real conversation with – and I'm pretty confident I was – then I could take this as an opportunity. Not to educate him out of his ignorance – that is very definitely not any 'onlys' job! – but to shift a perception through a small, insignificant interaction. Because my power as the only brown person he had talked to meant I could use that power to stand out in an idiocy-busting way.

Look, I'm not naive enough to think that my one passing conversation with this stranger will have shifted his world view forever but at least I shifted it for a moment. And maybe that moment will last or maybe it won't. But I did what I could to move the broader social conversation just that tiny millimetre forward. And that is the power of being the only. Because when we stand out, when the attention is on us because of some aspect of our identity, we can channel that attention to the things that others might not see. And maybe, hopefully, change things for the better for ourselves and others.

When I was the only person on my team whose name kept being butchered by my bosses at the Agency, I made a point to correct them, and then they made a point to learn how to say other non-white-American names properly, too. My being the only 'Rupal' (not Rupaul or Rupaal or Rupert) allowed me to make things just a little less awkward for all of my bosses' 'funny'-named colleagues to come.

When I was the only woman at a networking event for investors, I made a point to point out my only-ness and opened the event organizers' eyes to ways they could open their doors to other women investors, too. My being the only woman allowed me to make things just a little less difficult for all of the women investors to come.

When I was the only woman in a tent full of seasoned Special Forces tough guys in a remote outpost, I made a point to demonstrate how comfortable and tough I was in their habitat. My being the only civilian analyst twenty-something woman among them allowed me to use my bearing, my confidence and my intellectual rigour to make things just a little less forbidding for their future women colleagues to come.

All of these little interactions, these potential friction points where we can choose to ignore or acknowledge our only-ness add up. And if we don't use our power to chip away at stale, stereotypical notions, then the glaring neon signs that tell other people 'like us' to stay out, stay away and stay small remain firmly plugged in.

So when you are the only, yes, please acknowledge all of the baggage and pressure and scrutiny that comes with it but also acknowledge the power and the opportunity and the potential for change – for dimming the neon lights, as it were – that comes with it too.

Make Excuses or Make Things Happen

And while we are acknowledging our power, here's a reminder of the power our expectations and standards have.

At the start of every year, I find myself having lots of tough-love conversations with clients around their plans for their careers, their lives and their goals for the year ahead. The 'toughness' lies in encouraging (forcing!) them to expect more from themselves. Not to overburden themselves with self-flagellating demands but to set the bar just a little bit higher so they can prove to themselves that they are capable of more than they might have otherwise let themselves believe. (Basically, I have my version of 'what happened to the other two points' conversations with them; thank you, Mom and Dad!) I do this because human beings are notoriously responsive to expectations. We rise or fall to what is expected of us and to what we expect of ourselves. And that's why we regularly need to shake ourselves and remind ourselves that we can either make excuses or we can make things happen.

This is always true.

After my first daughter was born, I ran a business full-time and held investor meetings or important phone calls while breastfeeding. After a health complication, I went for daily hour-plus walks because I needed time away from the gym to recuperate but didn't want to give up on my body. After a major financial shock, I mercilessly eliminated costs in my personal life and businesses and got hustling to make more money. I take a shower every day (yes, even during lockdown!). I make my bed no matter how busy I am. My house is as tidy each night as I want it to be. And it doesn't matter if I am sick, postpartum or just damned tired, I have some key, basic standards that I never let myself lower.

But I am not a machine. I make choices (there's that word again) – choosing self-respect over self-sacrifice, self-care over self-pity, self-preservation over self-destruction. And I say this not because I am superhuman in any way but because I am very normal. I am just like you.

You have done the same. You have persevered when you wanted to give up. You have fought on when you wanted to let go. You have found a way forward when it would have been easier to float backward. You have made proactive and productive choices in different parts of your life at different times in your life. You did that. And I'm here to remind you of your own power because it's so easy to think others are better, more resilient, smarter working or luckier than we are. But that's not (usually) true. You can make choices that make you better, more resilient, smarter work-ing or luckier, too. You can choose to stop letting excuses stop you. Because otherwise, you will become resentful. Towards your children, your partner, your job – whatever it is you are using as an excuse to give up on yourself and your Mission. And resentment is not a good look.

Whenever you find yourself telling yourself you can't do something (i.e., making an excuse), choose to ask yourself instead 'how could I . . . ?' Let the question open up new choices that you hadn't let yourself see before.

With each passing year that flies by faster than the one before, I've started to see that there is literally no time for excuses. None at all. There is so much to do. So much to experience. So much to read and hear and see and discover – externally and internally. And there is no time to waste.

So stop making excuses and start making things happen.

Executive Order: Now, look, I know the same choices are not available to every one of us. Depending on who we are, where we live, our background and our social and personal context, our choice architecture is vastly different to and maybe vastly more limited than someone else's. I am not blind to the harshness of reality and that some of us have more circumscribed choices than others.

> But are you making the most of the choices you *do* have available to you? (Choosing an apple instead of a brownie, choosing a standing desk instead of a sitting one, choosing a partner who brings out the best in you instead of the person you're with when you're ready to settle down . . .) Because if not, you need to start. There is no room in your Mission or your life for excuses or self-pitying defeatism, so do the best you can with the choices you have available. The best you can. That's all.

The Art of the Possible

The great thing about choices is that we often have more available to us than we realize, but we need to practise the Art of the Possible to see them.

For so much of our lives, we are given messages around lack and scarcity and competition and winner-takes-all and zero-sum games and are made to feel that if someone else has already done something, it's not worth our bothering. But reality isn't like this. Sure, there are some things in life that are genuinely scarce: the element astatine (yes, I googled that), opportunities to walk on the moon, endangered animals like pikas (googled that too) and women at the top of pretty much every field you can think of. But many, many other things are not. And it's only once we start having a more abundant mindset that we will see that one person's success doesn't predetermine our stasis, that one person's beauty doesn't diminish our own, that one person's wealth doesn't subject us to poverty and that one person's critical acclaim doesn't deem us unworthy.

Instead of saying to ourselves *'All the clients are gone'*, *'All the good partners are already taken'*, *'All the positions I want are filled'*, *'All the art has already been created'*, we can start asking *'Where can I find the right clients for my unique offering?'*, *'Where can I find a mate who will bring out the best in me?'*, *'How can I expand my job search to find a perfect fit?'*, *'How can I create art that is different or unique?'* (Spoiler alert: everything you do will be unique because there is no other you out there.)

Do you see how the first is a set of statements, declarative and fixed, that focus our minds on scarcity and lack? And do you see how the second is a set of questions, open-ended and expansive, that challenge our minds to think creatively and abundantly . . . and imagine new possibilities?

What a huge difference.

Practising the Art of the Possible requires you to stop saying or doing something from a place of lack or limitation, stop telling yourself that you can't be/do/have something because someone else already is/does/has that thing, and to retrain your brain away from 'this is impossible' to 'how can I make this possible?'. You will need to be tactically ignorant and focus on what can be done instead of on what someone has deemed can't be, even if that 'someone' is the voice in your own head.

I've said it before but everything is at least theoretically possible – yes, even for you – so look for ways to make the theory real. Go back to basics. Lean on your Ops Team. Curate your mental and social environment. Surround yourself with doers and makers instead of talkers and consumers.

The Art of the Possible requires you to pull together **all** of the tools you've picked up during our time together and put them to use so you stop saying 'I can't do X . . .' and start asking 'how *can* I do X . . . ?' – and then make X happen.

If you had to find £10,000 to pay for a loved one's life-saving surgery, you wouldn't say *'Oh, that's impossible'* and give up on them; you would ask yourself *'How can I make ten grand?'* and then overturn every rock and pebble and sofa cushion to make that £10,000. If you had to quit your job to save your own life, you wouldn't say *'I can't do that, I'll just resign myself to my fate'*; you'd ask yourself *'How can I make a switch?'* and then call every person in your network to find a way to make the move. These are extreme examples but so often extremes (like we found during our Three Ideals exercises in Chapter 3) can illuminate a world of possibilities.

Indulge me for a second and ask yourself those two questions above right now. See for yourself what happens when you give your brain a question instead of a foregone conclusion. Questions create an insatiable requirement for answers, so your brain will kick into gear and start coming up with or looking for answers, even when the question is theoretical. When you prime your brain with questions, it will look for solutions. Everywhere. And all the time.

So the next time you find yourself saying *'I could never'* or *'That's not doable'* , turn those statements into questions (*'How could I . . . ?'*, *'What is doable . . .?'*) and let your brain find new possibilities for making things happen for you and for your Mission.

Executive Order: In addition to asking yourself open-ended questions, you can use targeted leaks to hold yourself accountable to doing what you told yourself was 'impossible'. Say you want to start a business or learn how to fly or perform on Broadway; tell other people that you are starting a business, learning how to fly or going to perform on Broadway. Once you've put it out there, you will have to figure out how to make it happen or risk losing face, and no one likes to lose face. I've used targeted leaks to do everything from becoming an international speaker, to starting my own businesses, to writing this book. I told people what I was going to do and then I had to make it happen. So my brain and I figured out how.

It wasn't ever a straight-line, easy or totally conscious process, and it often took longer than I expected (or wanted!). But I made a start, I used my tradecraft, I deployed all the tools in my arsenal, I did all the things I've encouraged you to do and I made it happen. And – at the risk of repeating myself one more time – if I can do it, you can do it. Of course you can. If any one person can, every person can. It's up to you to figure out how *you* are going to make your own version of impossible possible. I've given you all the tools I've got. And now it's on you to use them.

So good luck, my friend but please get going. Life is too short. Choose to see what might be possible for you – yes, you – and then work to make it so. I will be cheering for you and looking forward to hearing all about your Mission successes.

Key Intel

- Ask yourself 'what happened to the other points?' and whether you are living up to your potential. Be willing to set higher standards for yourself.
- Toughen up and take constructive criticism from those qualified to give it so that you can become bigger, better, bolder.
- Instead of feeling burdened by being the 'only' – and what a burden it can be – treat it as an opportunity to make a positive impact and call attention to issues that

are important to you or to other people who don't have your position.

- You can make excuses or you can make things happen; do the best you can with the choices you have available to you.
- The Art of the Possible is about actively looking for ways to make things possible; no more fixed declarations, only open-ended questions.
- Anything is possible, even for you.

Part Three After-Action Review

Way back when we first started on our journey, I promised you that by the end of our time together you would be raring to burst through your chrysalis of bad-assery, and I can almost hear the crackling and cracking as you do so. Now that you have started to come out of the shadows, let yourself shine, rewrite the rules and use tactical ignorance to push yourself further than you thought possible. Own and enjoy the bigger, better, bolder version of yourself that you always knew was hiding inside.

But don't stop now. Success and fulfilling your potential are never owned, they are leased – to paraphrase a great saying – and the rent is due every day. So keep at it. Keep going. Every day. It won't be easy but nothing worth having ever is.

I've got one last bit of all-source wisdom to share with you to keep your momentum going, so don't hang up your cloak and dagger just yet . . .

Conclusion
Sustaining Your Ops

Congratulations! You are now a fully trained, Mission-accomplishing badass. But here's the kicker: the training never stops and you will need to remain vigilant. Because there will inevitably be times when you'll forget your hard-won tradecraft and get guilted into doing something that drains you, or start hanging out with negative people because you feel bad about saying 'no', or throw up your hands because things are taking too long, or tune into to Radio Station URSHT and let the DJ retune your brain, or fall back into any of the patterns of living and leading that have never done anything for you.

It happens. To all of us. But to regain or sustain your *CIA to CEO* momentum, you can Track Your Stats so you don't – as a former Agency boss of mine once put it – snatch defeat from the jaws of Mission victory.

Track Your Stats

'Why isn't anything HAPPENING?!' That was my exasperated woe-is-me refrain when I was first getting started on my first business. I was convinced that I was going to dozens of pre-qualified meetings, spending hours on the phone with potential partners and suppliers and pounding the pavement all day long to build my business. My days would end and I would be convinced that I had done all the right things but I never felt any satisfaction or accomplishment. What the hell was happening?! Where was my progress?! If I was doing as much as I thought, why wasn't I seeing any results? I needed an independent way of checking up on myself, so I started to Track My Stats.

On an Excel spreadsheet (this was the early 2010s, before I discovered Toggl, the time-tracking app I now use), I broke down my working day into 15-minute increments and put those times down column A. Then, for two weeks, I filled in what activities I was doing during those time slots in column B (*0830–0845: financial analysis; 0845–0900: plan phone call with Mr X; 1200–1245: lunch* . . . and so on for the whole day). I also quantified as many of my daily activities as I could (number of phone calls, number of meetings, etc.), and at the end of two weeks reviewed what my days and weeks actually looked like.

And my results made me want to vomit with disappointment.

Conclusion

The first problem was that, way back then, I was working from home. And as everyone who has now had some experience of #WFH appreciates, it is so, so easy to slip into time-hoovering distractions masked as 'little' chores: *'That pile of laundry is getting so big . . . I'll just start a load and then settle back down at my desk'*; *'I'm so hungry. Why don't I finally crack open that cookbook?'*; *'I'm allowed to take a tea break and so what if I descale the kettle first?'*; and on and on and on. Not to mention that before the world was doing it, working from home was barely respected as work. People assumed that because I was at home, I was also available to run errands or indulge in long lunches or frivolous daytime fun when the reality was that I WAS WORKING. (Or trying to, in between invitations and interruptions and infuriatingly bemused looks of 'how quaint, you think starting a business from your home office counts as working'!)

The second problem was that I didn't set targets for my days or weeks. Each day was a blank slate and I would sit down at my desk and then look for work to do instead of working off a plan. I'd make a few phone calls, do some research, make a few tweaks to my spreadsheets, respond to some emails and do whatever else fell into my path that day. My days had no structure. I was reacting to events instead of taking control of them.

When I started Tracking My Stats it was hugely eye opening. And while it was disappointing to see how much of my time was being spent (not invested), it was also a huge relief because suddenly I could see that my lack of results wasn't because I was unlucky or doomed to fail, it was because I was working obliquely and without a plan.

So I started creating a plan for the week, setting targets for my days and working to those plans and targets. The other stuff (eating, laundry, kettle cleaning) still got done but at the end of the day; my prime brain-time went towards the activities that would create business results.

Tracking My Stats gave me a concrete and objective picture of where my time was actually being invested or spent. I could look back at a day, a week, a year and see exact percentages and numbers of minutes being invested in business development, marketing, admin, etc. And I could use those stats to hold myself accountable against the targets I had set.

Within weeks of changing how I approached my days, I got my first breakthrough. But it was only because I took the time to be honest with myself and Track My Stats that I was able to course correct and save myself the stress and worry that came with wondering why nothing was happening. Instead of despairing about where the time was going, I now had honest and, most important, objective data.

We are often the worst at assessing ourselves. And we often get it really wrong. We suffer from recency bias. And availability bias. And self-preservation bias. We judge our performance based on what has just happened, what we can recall (and we forget a lot), and we tell ourselves stories to make ourselves feel better (*'I am working so hard all day long!'*). But objectively measuring what we are/are not doing each day will lead to surprising and useful insights. It still does for me, years after I've made Tracking My Stats a habit.

In some instances, I am way ahead of my game (a few years ago, when I was having a really bad week, I wanted to see where I was going off track and you know what? I wasn't. I had hit 50 per cent of my targets for the year by May!). And in other cases, I am doing far less than I think (like when I realized I was going to the gym only once a week, despite telling myself that I value my health).

The data changes everything: practically, emotionally and energetically.

Because when we are ahead, isn't it great to know that? We can breathe a little easier, stop stressing about how much always needs to be done and maybe even celebrate our successes or pat ourselves on the back (crazy talk, I know!). And when we are behind, isn't the data morale boosting in a counterintuitive way too? If we aren't seeing progress, isn't it better to use the data to tell us whether that's because we're not investing enough time on the important things or if it's because we're spending too much time on 'low-value' things? Isn't it better to know if the flaw is with the process or with the execution?

The data gives us answers. The data helps uncover solutions. And the data makes it easier to know instead of guess.

Because your Mission success won't happen by guesswork. So when you go off course – or even when you are steadily on course – swap the confusion of wondering with the power of knowing and Track Your Stats.

Things will get hard. And get on top of you. But Tracking Your Stats will help you build a baseline of expectations for how long certain things 'should' take. And then when things get tough and you feel like you're at a standstill, you can go back to your stats and say *'Oh! My last product launch took three weeks and four hours to take off, and I'm only in week two of my current launch, so I guess I don't totally suck at life, I just gotta stick it out for a few more days to get this launch in shape . . .'*

It might feel strange or 'too scientific' but gathering data about your time will support your Mission and keep you from quitting too soon when things get hard. Because that's what too many people do – they quit because they feel things are taking too long and then give up inches before striking gold – and I don't want you to become that kind of stat.

I see it so many times from the founders I work with who give up on making a new hire or getting admin support because 'it's taking too long to find a qualified candidate'. And then they struggle with burnout and wonder why staying 'Chief Everything Officer' isn't working.

I see it so many times from the corporate leaders I work with, who resist putting themselves out there because it

Conclusion

feels 'icky' and 'self-promotey' and their first LinkedIn post didn't immediately get 10,000 views. So they quit posting before they've really started and then wonder why they never get noticed for the right reasons and why they feel stuck in professional limbo.

And I see it so many times from the business school students I mentor who are trying to change careers or want to start their own businesses but give up because 'it takes too long to scale'. And then they wonder why they aren't happy when they go back to their previous careers and why they feel deflated and rudderless.

What I carefully and tactically remind them is that everything is hard before it gets easy. Everything starts out awkward and icky and scary and overwhelming. Everything worth having requires us to get comfortable with discomfort and to put in the hours and the right effort again and again and again. Tracking Your Stats will make sure you do so because you'll see objectively when you've only spent three hours looking at the CVs of potential hires instead of the three days it has felt like. You'll see objectively when you have only posted once on social media instead of the dozens of posts you swore you put out there because it feels so emotionally taxing to come out of the shadows. You'll see objectively that most businesses take years to grow and become profitable so if you've just thrown a few weekends at it, it's not enough. And the data is telling you it's not time to quit. There is more work to do.

So keep doing it. Track Your Stats, keep yourself honest and keep going before your window of opportunity closes on your Mission. Because we all know that it will, we just never know when . . .

Executive Order: Take the Ride

We've come full circle, talking about windows of opportunity again, so I'm going to close on a big-picture philosophical note that echoes why we got started on this journey together: because you know there is more for you, more in you, and you want to channel it, to bring it into the world and get out of your own way. You want to make the most of this one chance you've got at life and tap into that vast and deep potential you've kept buried inside. And you don't want to waste any more time because — if you're anything like me — you're finding that yes, the days might feel painfully long sometimes but the years are even more painfully short.

So let's end our wild ride together on a high that will keep you going higher.

A few years ago, I was standing in front of my closet looking for something to wear for a business trip to exotic Stoke-on-Trent (yes, even Stoke is exotic for an expat like me!) and out of the corner of my eye I caught sight of a hideously ugly dress that made me smile . . . and then guffaw.

The dress in question is an extra-wide A-line with puffy white sleeves, near-life-size faces of strangers

---

printed on the front and back and has two large slits at the back for a harness. Oh, and it's made of neoprene. Now, before you question my sanity or lifestyle choices for owning a dress that comes with harness slits, let me hasten to explain that it was the dress I wore for the opening ceremony of the London 2012 Olympics.

The ugliness of that dress makes it all the more endearing because from so much ugly came so much beauty: I became friends with three amazing creatives who were fellow volunteers and am still close friends with them now. And I got to be a part of a once-in-a-lifetime event in an up-close-and-personal way.

Being a volunteer for the London 2012 opening and closing ceremonies was one of the best adventures of my life, even though I spent that summer eating horrible boxed lunches instead of doing the 'smart' thing for my career, which would have been to get an internship with a top-tier consulting firm (I was an MBA student at the time).

But I didn't choose 'smart'; I chose adventure.

My dear readers, life literally gets shorter with each passing day and as high achievers with big ambitions and meaningful Missions, we can get so consumed with achieving and doing and Missioning that sometimes we can forget about the fun-for-its-own-sake. Sometimes we can forget that we need work *and* play (even when work already feels like play). And sometimes we can forget that adventure can come around every day if we are open to seeing it.

I'm not advocating hedonism or the mindless pursuit of novelty or throwing responsibility to the wind. What I am encouraging is that we at least consider saying yes the next time adventure comes by our door. It might come in the guise of a new business venture. Or a song idea. Or a trip to Nashville. Or a walk around that museum we pass every day. Or confessing to someone how we truly feel about them (good or bad!). Or having a conversation with a total stranger who strikes us as interesting.

Going on an adventure isn't about bungee jumping and skydiving; it's about finding the thrilling aspects of the things we encounter every day and letting ourselves be thrilled by them. It's about (at least sometimes) choosing joy over ROI. About saying yes sometimes when we might otherwise have said no. And for me, it's also about living the type of life that will take me on physical, emotional and mental rides and then letting myself feel the feels and enjoy the aliveness, even during the 'downs'.

Our time together has gone so quickly and so will yours on this amazing planet, so I'll leave you with one last thing to consider. As you get fully into this weekend, and next week, and next month, and next year, what adventure will you say yes to? What adventure will you allow into your life that will stretch you, grow you, nurture you or simply make you smile (then guffaw!) when you look inside your closet of life?

I'd love to hear all about it, neoprene and all.

Acknowledgements

As someone who reads the acknowledgements section of every book I finish (I mean does it count as reading the whole book if you skip pages??), I never thought it would be the hardest section to write. My I-owe-you-for's list is long and deep, so thank you in advance for your graciousness if I've inadvertently left you out in print. You know who you are, and I will make sure you feel my appreciation even if you don't read it here.

And for those of you who I've advertently put in print, these words are a fraction of my thanks, but I've tried to do you justice.

To my parents, thank you for always expecting more and seeing hidden potential in me and the world around us. Our family dinners during childhood were the source of much irritation and eye-rolling at the time (did 'normal' families do brain teasers and learn lessons in financial literacy over rotli and shaak, I often wondered . . .), but clearly your message and your powerful example had a massive and lasting impact. Being forged in our brand of Patel steel has been my personal jackpot win.

To 'us', our sibling foursome is another jackpot win, and I owe you each in big and small ways. Kush, for your magical ability to create time and for always showing up for me no matter the time difference or your lack of sleep. Sonal for soul-checking me and keeping me growing and expanding in ways I didn't realize I could or needed to. And Lava for being one of my earliest heroes and role models. You still are.

To my large extended family, and to the family I chose for myself, you might see echoes of our conversations in here, so thank you for being you. Extra special thanks to Paige, Brooke, Jacquie, and Polly, my original Ops Team, even though you might not have known it until now.

To Richard Brown and Helen Pollock who started a powerful chain reaction from that fateful podcast interview all those years ago. To my wonderful agent and fellow RENT-lover, Charlotte Colwill for getting me on so many levels and schooling me in the dark arts of publishing. To my editors Rik Ubhi and Justine Taylor for being such enthusiastic and terrifyingly insightful editors, and to the peerless Liz Marvin who makes my version of "detail-oriented" look quaint when compared to her eagle eyes and instinctive wordsmithing prowess. To Jenna Petts and Frankie Eades for your creativity and commitment to giving my work a bullhorn. You all

Acknowledgements

are – and hopefully will remain – the Dream Team of Book Publishing Ops Teams.

To Shonda Rhimes, Antii Tuomainen, and Anne Lamott who fuelled me in ways you can never know (because we don't know each other . . . but I would love to change that, hint hint!). Your work refuelled me during the draining (if life-giving) process of writing, and this book would be sucked of life – or maybe just suck! – if I hadn't been pumped back full by your work. Thank you.

And finally, to my husband, Guy: you are my slipstream, and your ten thousand did the world a favour by bringing your DNA into it.

And finally, finally, to my two magical, star-dust-made little creatures: you are my heart and soul's mitochondria.

A Note on the Dedication

As you've seen from our time together, I love analysis. I love knowledge. I am a life-long learner. I try to understand. To dissect. To get back to first principles. And I recognize that who I am is a product of many, many streams of 'All-Source Intel'.

There are people who have left a mark on me, on my DNA, and who contributed to who I am because they left their mark on other people, on all the people I come from. My lineage, like everyone else's, is made up of thousands and thousands of unknowable people, and thousands and thousands of unknowable interactions. We are all the results of an unbroken chain of creation and evolution and survival that has remained unbroken for billions of years. Billions. Of. Years.

And that is why this book is dedicated to 'my ten thousand'. My ten thousand are the ancestors I have never met, the people who fought their way through life, the hunter-